KW-481-631

Workbook 1

STP Caribbean Mathematics

FOURTH EDITION

S Chandler
E Smith

OXFORD

Great Clarendon Street, Oxford, OX2 6DP, United Kingdom

Oxford University Press is a department of the University of Oxford.
It furthers the University's objective of excellence in research, scholarship,
and education by publishing worldwide. Oxford is a registered trade mark of
Oxford University Press in the UK and in certain other countries

First published by Nelson Thornes Ltd in 2012
This edition published by Oxford University Press in 2020

British Library Cataloguing in Publication Data
Data available

978-0-19-842651-6

10 9 8 7 6 5 4 3 2 1

Printed and bound by CPI Group (UK) Ltd, Croydon, CR0 4YY

Acknowledgements

Cover image: Radachynskyi/iStock

Although we have made every effort to trace and contact all
copyright holders before publication this has not been possible in all
cases. If notified, the publisher will rectify any errors or omissions at
the earliest opportunity.

Links to third party websites are provided by Oxford in good faith
and for information only. Oxford disclaims any responsibility for
the materials contained in any third party website referenced in
this work.

Contents

Answers to the questions in this book can be found on your free support website. Access your support website here: **www.oxfordsecondary.com/9780198426516**

1   Whole number arithmetic

1 Write these numbers in figures:

a seven hundred and sixty-four   _____

b twenty-seven thousand and forty _____

c thirty million and fourteen _____

d ten million nine hundred thousand

_____

2 Write in words:

a 293 _____

b 6276 _____

c 745 600 _____

d 5 400 000 _____

e 3 004 005 _____

3 Look at the number 3 506 309. Write the digit that gives:

a the number of thousands   _____

b the number of millions   _____

c the number of hundred thousands. _____

4 Look at the number 215 673 498. Write the digit that gives:

a the number of tens   _____

b the number of thousands   _____

c the number of millions   _____

d the number of hundred millions. _____

5 Write these numbers in order with the smallest first:

74 562, 9983, 9365, 10 754, 9193

_____

6 Write these numbers in order, smallest first:

8823, 18 222, 7363, 999, 9283, 10 065

_____

7 Write these numbers in order with the largest first:

67 328, 46 132, 123 943, 9456, 88 335

_____

8 Write these numbers in order with the largest first:

834 632, 773 345, 93 949, 1 745 547, 814 756

_____

9 Write the value of the digit 3 in these numbers:

a 582 371   _____

b 6 300 400   _____

c 23 478 900   _____

10 Write the value of the digit 7 in these numbers:

a 982 371   _____

b 6 370 200   _____

c 27 418 900   _____

11

Use all five cards to make:

a the largest number possible   _____

b the smallest number possible.   _____

12

Use all five cards to make:

a the largest number possible   _____

b the smallest number possible.   _____

13

1	7	0
3	2	5

Use all six cards to make:

a the largest number possible _____

b the smallest number possible. _____

14 Use each of the digits 8, 0, 5, 3, 1 once to make the smallest possible number.

_____

15 Use each of the digits 7, 6, 8, 0, 5, 3 once to make the largest possible number.

_____

16 Look at these numbers:

i thirty-one thousand and sixteen

ii thirty-one thousand and seven.

Which is the larger? _____

17 Look at these numbers:

i three thousand and eighty-four

ii fourteen hundred and seventy.

Which is the larger? _____

18 Look at these numbers:

i sixteen thousand four hundred

ii one hundred and four thousand and three.

Which is the smaller? _____

19 Look at these numbers:

i eighty-four thousand and seventeen

ii two hundred thousand six hundred and fifty.

Which is the smaller? _____

20 Find the value of:

a 5 + 6 + 3 + 7 _____

b 8 + 4 + 5 + 3 + 4 _____

c 3 + 8 + 7 + 5 + 6 + 6 _____

d 7 + 8 + 1 + 5 + 2 + 9 _____

21 Find the value of:

a 4 + 6 + 7 + 7 _____

b 8 + 9 + 5 + 3 + 4 _____

c 3 + 8 + 7 + 7 + 6 + 6 _____

d 7 + 8 + 9 + 5 + 5 + 3 _____

22 Find the value of:

a 45	**b** 37	**c** 32	**d** 74
25	45	67	62
52	32	96	34
+17	+66	+31	+54

23 Find the value of:

a 65	**b** 37	**c** 82	**d** 34
71	86	49	44
25	45	67	62
32	72	26	84
+19	+76	+36	+55

24 Find the value of:

a 6341	**b** 6677	**c** 2962	**d** 8834
2055	4225	6897	3962
+9237	+4366	+3721	+9214

25 Find the value of:

a 65	**b** 37	**c** 82	**d** 34
71	86	49	44
25	45	67	62
32	72	26	84
+19	+76	+36	+55

26 Find the value of:

a 3065	**b** 9237	**c** 10182	**d** 300654
10882	34598	504067	452062
9683	20782	277006	286540
+4419	+7386	+35600	+55773

27 Find the value of:

   a 3308 + 690 + 432 _____

   b 56 000 + 40 052 + 29 040 _____

   c 75 000 + 540 000 + 40 053 _____

28 Find the value of:

   a 48 308 + 6907 + 40 032 _____

   b 256 000 + 10 052 + 269 020 _____

   c 55 008 + 354 200 + 10 073 _____

29 Find the value of:

   a 123 7300 + 20 690 + 54 436

   _____

   b 1 156 000 + 90 058 + 20 903 840

   _____

   c 75 000 200 + 14 005 500 + 1 409 052

   _____

30 Add five hundred and sixty seven, four hundred and thirteen and five thousand and seven.

_____

31 Add fifteen hundred and six, one thousand and twenty, and six hundred and nine.

_____

32 Find the cost of three food packs costing $743, $933 and $1734.

_____

33 Find the total cost of a lawnmower priced at $2860, a hedgecutter priced at $1449 and a set of garden tools priced at $189.

_____

34 Find the total cost of an electric saw at $1550, a set of chisels at $320 and a woodwork manual costing $350.

_____

35 When Jade bought her new curtains, which cost $4490, she also bought bed linen costing $950 and a cushion priced at $750. How much did she spend altogether?

_____

36 Add seven thousand and fifty-six, two thousand and four, and eleven thousand seven hundred and thirty-three.

_____

37 Add five hundred thousand, three hundred and sixteen to eighty-four thousand, nine hundred and five.

_____

38 Exits along a section of a Freeway are numbered from 6 to 57. How many exits are there in this section of the Freeway?

_____

39 Bella has four lengths of a particular curtain material. Their lengths are 576 mm, 395 mm, 446 mm and 174 mm.

   a What is the length of the longest and

      shortest pieces? _____

   b What is the total length of the two shortest

      pieces? _____

   c What length of this material does she have

      altogether? _____

40 Mandy goes shopping with $5000. In the first shop she spends $1490. In the second shop she spends $1884, and in the third shop her bill comes to $1656. Does she have enough money? Justify your answer.

_____

41 After Grant drops his children off at school, which is 2700 m from home, he drives on to visit his parents some 5750 m from the school. After spending an hour with his parents he drives the 6500 m home. Later in the day he drives to school to pick up his children and bring them home. How far has he driven altogether?

_____

42 Last year, during the first six months of the year, the numbers visiting a zoo were 1649, 2423, 4621, 12 047, 27 267 and 35 937. Find the total number of visitors to the zoo during this period.

_____

43 During the last week of January, the number of new cars imported into the Caribbean by the main dealers were: Monday 934, Tuesday 1026, Wednesday 1139, Thursday 1243, Friday 976. How many cars were imported during the week?

_____

44 Find:

a $54 - 36$ _____ **b** $76 - 32$ _____

c $85 - 77$ _____ **d** $345 - 187$ _____

e $645 - 522$ _____ **f** $836 - 532$ _____

45 Find:

a $8659 - 6335$ _____

b $66\,006 - 34\,607$ _____

c $304\,721 - 180\,065$ _____

d $900\,532 - 740\,038$ _____

e $43\,070\,000 - 36\,000\,000$ _____

f $734\,000\,000 - 602\,050\,500$ _____

46 Put + or − in each box so that the calculations are correct.

a $14 \square 8 \square 6 = 12$

b $8 \square 9 \square 16 \square 5 = 6$

c $17 \square 3 \square 8 \square 4 = 24$

47 Put + or − in each box so that the calculations are correct.

a $12 \square 6 \square 3 = 15$

b $7 \square 3 \square 12 \square 14 = 2$

c $21 \square 7 \square 4 \square 9 = 15$

d $25 \square 8 \square 4 \square 3 \square 7 = 17$

48 The workforce in a factory is 1264. If there are 573 men how many women are there?

_____

49 Take five thousand and thirty-three away from seven thousand three hundred and six.

_____

50 The combined population of Sandford and Rockford is 36 782. If 18 053 live in Sandford, find:

a the population of Rockford

_____

b how many more people live in Rockford than in Sandford.

_____

51 Complete these equations by adding the missing figure:

a $67 - 44 = \square 3$ _____

b $49 + 37 = \square 6$ _____

c $83 - \square 5 = 48$ _____

d $35 + 43 = \square 8$ _____

e $\square 7 - 62 = 25$ _____

52 Find:

    a 43 – 37 + 11 – 3   _____

    b 56 + 71 – 87 – 13   _____

    c 317 – 166 + 84 – 56   _____

    d 981 – 672 + 331 – 422   _____

53 Find:

    a 27 – 16 – 4 + 8   _____

    b 54 + 17 – 43 – 6   _____

    c 39 – 12 – 9 + 72   _____

    d 83 – 51 + 43 – 62   _____

54 Find:

    a 38 – 19 + 7 – 8   _____

    b 84 + 36 – 43 – 15   _____

    c 26 – 12 – 5 + 57   _____

    d 93 – 72 + 34 – 43   _____

55 Find:

    a 229 – 216 – 74 + 68   _____

    b 745 + 187 – 463 – 17   _____

    c 569 – 128 – 94 + 553   _____

    d 483 – 351 + 463 – 165   _____

56 Find:

    a 5329 – 2176 – 3554 + 683   _____

    b 8745 + 1537 – 4669 – 1337   _____

    c 2569 – 1244 – 947 + 5233   _____

    d 3563 – 3006 + 4265 – 2168   _____

57 Find:

    a 20 232 – 1213 – 16 748 + 3608

    _____

    b 574 000 + 641 087 – 436 003 – 160 700

    _____

    c 28 004 690 – 17 280 500 – 840 000 + 755 000

    _____

    d 75 000 600 + 845 000 – 53 000 000 + 14 600 300

    _____

58 A teacher has to mark 76 Grade 7 exercise books, 56 Grade 8 exercise books and 84 Grade 9 exercise books. What is the total number of books that the teacher has to mark?

_____

59 What is the difference in the value of the two 8s in the number 84 831?

_____

60 49 students go on a school trip. There are 5 more girls than boys. How many boys are there?

_____

61 Telegraph poles are placed at 50 metre intervals. The last pole on a stretch of road is 2150 metres from the first. How many poles are there?

_____

62 Find the difference between two thousand and sixty seven, and nine hundred and eighty-three. Then add on fifty-four.

_____

63 Subtract two hundred and forty-seven from eleven hundred and four. Now add on forty-eight.

_____

64 Deron has 166 boxes of eggs, each of which is packed with six eggs.

    a How many eggs are there altogether in these boxes? _____

    b His customer wants 1000 eggs. How many eggs is he short? _____

65 Rohan buys a 10 000 cm long ball of string. He cuts off three pieces: one 354 cm long, a second 175 cm long and a third 240 cm long.

a What is the total length of string has Rohan cut off?

_____

b What length remains?

_____

66 The air miles between four cities are:

Washington to Chicago 607

Chicago to Sydney 9241

Sydney to Rome 10153

Rome to Chicago 4821

Washington to Sydney 9804

Rome to Washington 4485

a An American diplomat has to make a round trip from Washington calling at Chicago, Rome and Sydney in that order. How many miles does he fly?

_____

b When he is in Chicago he receives a call to tell him to miss Rome and fly direct to Sydney. By how many miles is his trip shortened?

_____

c Which is the shorter round trip from Washington and by how much:

i Rome and back, or

ii Sydney and back calling at Chicago on both the outward and inward journeys?

_____

67 The ages of the workforce in a large factory are given as:

1761 are under the age of 21, 6283 are under the age of 40, 10 440 are under the age of 60 and 2764 are 60 or over.

How many people are:

a employed at the factory

_____

b aged under 40 but at least 22

_____

c aged between 21 and 60?

_____

68 Deliveries to and from a supermarket warehouse, of tins of its own brand of baked beans, are listed in the table.

	Mon	Tues	Wed	Thurs	Fri	Sat	Sun
Received	864	1152	384	432	240	672	0
Distributed	576	1056	912	816	768	624	0

a If there were 720 tins in the warehouse before the Monday deliveries, how many tins:

i were received during the week?

_____

ii were distributed to its stores during the week?

_____

iii were in the warehouse when it opened on Wednesday?

_____

iv were in the warehouse when it closed on Thursday?

_____

b Was there any day when all the outgoing deliveries could not be fulfilled until their incoming orders had been made? Explain your answer.

_____

69 Write each of the following numbers as an approximate number of tens.

a 72 _____ **b** 37 _____

c 535 _____ **d** 2188 _____

70 Write each of the following numbers as an approximate number of hundreds.

a 526 _____ **b** 7672 _____

c 2450 _____ **d** 8497 _____

71 Write each of the following numbers as an approximate number of thousands.

a 40982 _____ **b** 734944 _____

c 878483 _____ **d** 2588749 _____

72 Write each of the following numbers as an approximate number of tens of thousands.

a 167364 _____ **b** 657938 _____

c 763883 _____ **d** 307288 _____

73 Write each of the following numbers as an approximate number of millions.

a 7563523 _____ **b** 6633798 _____

c 15416532 _____ **d** 85635040 _____

In questions **74** to **77**, write each number correct to the nearest number of 10s and find an approximate answer.

74 a $127 + 279$ _____

b $37 + 122 + 84$ _____

c $13 + 95 + 127$ _____

75 a $52 - 29$ _____

b $413 - 269$ _____

c $1641 - 988$ _____

76 a $321 + 295 - 463$ _____

b $49 + 52 + 67 + 34 + 19$ _____

77 a $121 + 47 + 228 - 172$ _____

b $342 - 183 + 95 - 147$ _____

78 Find:

a 47×4 _____

b 17×9 _____

c 207×3 _____

d 7×37 _____

79 Find:

a 69×10 _____

b 14×100 _____

c 83×1000 _____

d 67×10000 _____

80 Find:

a 73×200 _____

b 47×70 _____

c 304×50 _____

d 666×300 _____

81 Find:

a 504×20 _____

b 664×80 _____

c 270×400 _____

d 542×600 _____

82 Find:

a 812×5000 _____

b 21212×900 _____

c 400×7921 _____

d 7000×5362 _____

Use a calculator for questions **83** and **84**.

83 Find:

a 901×7060 _____

b 3630×6200 _____

c 35200×1025 _____

d 62008×2050 _____

84 Find:

   a $56\,007 \times 250\,040$ _____

   b $30\,450 \times 54\,002$ _____

   c $73\,008 \times 4060$ _____

   d $40\,510 \times 80\,701$ _____

85 Estimate each answer. Then use a calculator to work out the following:

   a 49×51 _____

   b 157×98 _____

   c 307×104 _____

   d 721×29 _____

86 Estimate each answer. Then use a calculator to work out the following:

   a 285×64 _____

   b 4545×567 _____

   c 3214×5432 _____

   d 6758×3766 _____

87 Estimate each answer. Then use a calculator to work out the following:

   a 885×2645 _____

   b 545×3567 _____

   c 7074×9875 _____

   d 1267×6673 _____

88 Estimate each answer. Then use a calculator to work out the following:

   a 8624×5324 _____

   b 5099×3072 _____

   c 2865×7009 _____

   d 9803×7068 _____

89 In a book, chapter 7 begins on page 254 and ends on page 291. How many pages are in this chapter?

_____

90 The house numbers on one side of a street in Freetown have consecutive odd numbers. They start at 47 and end at 79. How many houses are there on that side of the street?

_____

91 Tim thinks of a number. He chooses 13. How many times must he add 17 to it to get a number greater than 100?

_____

92 Parties of pupils from several schools are taken to a concert. The first school takes 345 students, the second school takes 176 students and the third school takes 254 students.

   a How many students are taken to the concert?

   _____

   b The venue has 950 seats. How many spare seats are there?

   _____

93 Angela's first novel has 256 pages. She estimates that each page has 34 lines and each line has 12 words.

   a Estimate:

    i the number of words on one page

    _____

    ii the number of words in the book.

    _____

   b The publishing company ask her to reduce the length of the book to $65\,000$ words.

   About how many pages would she have to remove?

   _____

94 Find the cost of two bicycles costing $2675 each and three safety helmets costing $255 each.

_____

95 Do the following calculations and give the remainder where there is one:

a   48 ÷ 3   _____

b   88 ÷ 5   _____

c   67 ÷ 5   _____

d   59 ÷ 4   _____

96 Do the following calculations and give the remainder where there is one:

a   236 ÷ 8   _____

b   665 ÷ 6   _____

c   785 ÷ 7   _____

d   923 ÷ 9   _____

97 Do the following calculations and give the remainder where there is one:

a   6064 ÷ 4   _____

b   8234 ÷ 9   _____

c   1764 ÷ 8   _____

d   3373 ÷ 7   _____

98 Do the following calculations and give the remainder where there is one:

a   806 046 ÷ 6   _____

b   152 345 ÷ 5   _____

c   2 741 764 ÷ 8   _____

d   7 077 077 ÷ 3   _____

99 Do the following calculations and give the remainder where there is one:

a   67 ÷ 3   _____

b   84 ÷ 9   _____

c   384 ÷ 7   _____

d   927 ÷ 5   _____

e   4837 ÷ 8   _____

f   1737 ÷ 4   _____

100 Do the following calculations and give the remainder where there is one:

a   750 ÷ 100   _____

b   23 ÷ 10   _____

c   5634 ÷ 100   _____

d   4892 ÷ 1000   _____

e   644 ÷ 100   _____

f   9093 ÷ 10   _____

g   1734 ÷ 100   _____

101 Do the following calculations and give the remainder where there is one:

a   573 ÷ 24   _____

b   623 ÷ 50   _____

c   3285 ÷ 73   _____

d   9732 ÷ 800   _____

e   264 ÷ 36   _____

f   8909 ÷ 58   _____

g   1945 ÷ 46   _____

102 Do the following calculations and give the remainder where there is one:

a   734 ÷ 21   _____

b   283 ÷ 45   _____

c   3774 ÷ 37   _____

d   6936 ÷ 640   _____

e   564 ÷ 53   _____

f   9990 ÷ 34   _____

g   1553 ÷ 88   _____

103 Find:

a $7 + 6 \times 3 - 10$ _____

b $4 \times 9 - 17$ _____

c $16 \div 4 + 8 \times 3$ _____

d $5 \times 8 - 8 + 7 \times 3$ _____

e $15 \div 5 + 6 \times 3 - 14$ _____

f $7 \times 2 - 21 \div 7 + 5$ _____

g $18 \div (11 - 2) \times 5 - 6$ _____

104 Find:

a $2 \times 15 \div 10 + 8$ _____

b $5 \times 8 \div 10 + 10$ _____

c $8 - 12 \div 3 - 2$ _____

105 Find:

a $24 \div 6 + 2 \times 5$ _____

b $4 \times 4 \div 16 + 1$ _____

c $9 \div 3 + 12 \div 4 - 5$ _____

106 Find:

a $2 \times 3 \times 4 \div 8 + 5 - 2$ _____

b $6 + 5 \times 3 - 12 \div 3 + 15 \div 5$ _____

c $9 + 9 \div 3 + 4 \times 2 - 8 \div 2$ _____

d $8 \times 4 - 3 \times 2 \times 4 - 12 \div 3$ _____

107 Find:

a $24 \div 8 + 5 \times 2 - 12 \div 2$ _____

b $9 - 32 \div 4 + 8 \div 2$ _____

c $20 \div 5 - 27 \div 9 + 3 \times 5$ _____

d $36 \div 9 + 4 \times 3 - 2 \times 8$ _____

108 Find:

a $15 \div (8 - 3)$ _____

b $3 + 4 \times (2 + 7)$ _____

c $2 \times (9 - 4) \div (8 - 3)$ _____

d $(3 + 4) \times 2 + 12 \div (7 - 3)$ _____

e $(45 - 8 + 14) \div 3$ _____

f $(55 \div 11) - (24 \div 6)$ _____

g $(21 - 13) \div (17 - 1) \times 8$ _____

109 Find:

a $24 \div (11 - 3)$ _____

b $(27 - 13) \div (13 - 6)$ _____

c $(33 \div 11) + (36 \div 9)$ _____

d $(56 \div 8) - (36 \div 9)$ _____

e $(7 - 2) \times 3 + 20 \div (8 - 3)$ _____

f $5 \times (12 - 7) \div (9 \times 3 - 2)$ _____

g $(13 - 7 + 9) \div (12 \div 4)$ _____

h $(25 - 19) \div (17 - 3) \times 7$ _____

i $(14 - 9) \times 4 - 30 \div (9 - 4)$ _____

j $(23 - 15) \div (13 - 9) \times 4$ _____

110 Which is the larger, and by how much?

a 19×20 or 21×18 _____

b 14×9 or 10×13 _____

c 43×6 or 8×34 _____

d 57×7 or 43×9 _____

111 Which is the smaller, and by how much?

a 16×23 or 21×17 _____

b 15×11 or 10×16 _____

c 33×9 or 8×37 _____

d 87×7 or 72×9 _____

112 Which is the larger and by how much?

a 20×21 or 22×19 _____

b 13×8 or 9×12 _____

c 37×7 or 33×8 _____

d 64×6 or 7×54 _____

113 Which is the smaller and by how much?

a 32×9 or 34×7 _____

b 12×16 or 14×15 _____

c 49×8 or 9×41 _____

d 56×8 or 62×7 _____

114 How many times can 37 be taken away from 750?

_____

115 How many times can 54 be taken away from 900?

_____

116 Asif's salary is $13 440 for working four five-day weeks every month.

  a How much does Asif earn:

    i each week _____

    ii each day? _____

  b Assuming that he works 8 hours every day calculate his hourly rate of pay.

    _____

  c If Asif works a 52-week year, and is paid at the same weekly rate as you have calculated above, calculate his annual salary.

    _____

117 On consecutive Saturdays the attendances at the Emirates stadium were 67 434 and 65 878. Find the decrease in attendance.

_____

118 In a large school there are 136 fewer students this year than last year, and it is expected that there will be a further fall of 74 students next year. If there are 1492 students in the school this year, calculate the number of students:

  a in the school last year

    _____

  b expected to be in the school next year.

    _____

119 In a factory with a workforce consisting of 365 men, 386 women and 121 young people, 727 are paid a weekly wage while the remainder receive an annual salary. How many are paid an annual salary?

_____

120 A soccer player estimates that he runs 15 kilometres during a match. He plays twice a week in a thirty-six week season. Find the total distance he has run during the season.

_____

121 On a particular day, a supermarket sold 76 large packets of ginger biscuits, 47 medium-sized packets and 82 small packets. If a large packet contains 36 biscuits, a medium packet 24 biscuits and a small packet 18 biscuits, how many biscuits were sold on that day?

_____

122 At a concert, 247 seats were sold at $75 each, 534 at $45 each and 413 at $35 each. Find the total amount of money taken for all the seats.

_____

123 There are 1428 students in a school with a teaching staff of 84. How many pupils is this for each teacher?

_____

124 Muffins are packed three to a box.

  a How many boxes are needed to pack 655 muffins?

    _____

  b How many extra muffins are needed to fill the last box?

    _____

125 A factory produces 3545 car wheels in a week. If each car needs 5 wheels, how many cars can be fitted with one week's production of wheels?

_____

126 How many years, each with 365 days, are there in 16 425 days?

_____

127 There are 321 516 voters in the County of Roxborough. For local elections, the county is divided into regions, each region having 2748 voters. How many regions are there in the County of Roxborough?

_____

128 A bookseller has 42 packets of a new book. Each packet contains 24 books. He stores them on shelves in his shop. How many shelves are needed if each shelf will house 56 books?

_____

129 Thirty-two children in a class collect tokens in order to send for games that are advertised on a cornflakes packet. Each child collects 17 tokens. If each game requires 50 tokens, how many games would the class be able to send for?

_____

In questions **130** to **138**, write down the next two numbers in the pattern:

130 2, 5, 8, 11, _____

131 20, 17, 14, 11, _____

132 9, 16, 25, 36, _____

133 64, 32, 16, 8, _____

134 2, 6, 12, 20, _____

135 5, 12, 19, 26, _____

136 60, 50, 39, 27, _____

137 15, 17, 20, 24, _____

138 100, 95, 89, 82, 74, _____

139 Which of the following are square numbers?

2, 4, 8, 16, 30, 49, 53, 72, 80, 101, 121

_____

140 Which of the following are square numbers?

3, 9, 14, 20, 25, 32, 39, 64, 81, 93, 125

_____

141 Which of the following are rectangular numbers?

8, 13, 16, 19, 30, 49, 53, 71, 80, 101, 121

_____

142 Which of the following are rectangular numbers?

7, 10, 18, 23, 29, 32, 59, 79, 81, 96

_____

143 Show that:

a 16 is a rectangular number in two different ways

_____

b 24 is a rectangular number in three different ways

_____

c 48 is a rectangular number in four different ways.

_____

144 Which of the following are **not** triangular numbers? Give a reason for your answer.

7, 15, 23, 36, 47, 56

_____

145 Using the signs $+ - \times$ and $\div$, four 3s can be used to make all the numbers from 0 to 10.

For example: $\dfrac{3+3+3}{3} = 3$ and $3 \times 3 - \dfrac{3}{3} = 8$.

Using exactly four 3s each time, make the other numbers from 0 to 10.

_____

_____

_____

146 Now try the same question using four 2s. It may not be possible for all numbers.

_____

_____

_____

147 Write the numbers between 20 and 30 that are:

a square numbers _____

b rectangular numbers _____

c triangular numbers. _____

In questions **148** and **149**, complete the magic squares. Use the digits 1 to 9 just once in each square. The numbers in every row, in every column and in each diagonal should add up to 15. Use a pencil in case you need to rub out.

148

6		8
	5	
		4

149

	1	
	5	
	9	4

In questions **150** and **151**, copy and complete the magic square. Use the digits 1 to 16 just once in each square. The numbers in every row, in every column and in each diagonal should add up to 34. Use a pencil in case you need to rub out.

150

2		7	11
15	3	10	
9			
		1	

151

13	1		8
	16	5	9
	7		2

152 Gerrard get paid $1250 for a five-day working week. How much is this per day?

_____

153 Stamps come in sheets of 200.

a What is the value of a sheet of 25c stamps?

_____

b What is the value of a sheet of 75c stamps?

_____

154 Frances has 1900 cents. She buys as many ballpoint pens as she can at 45c each.

a How many pens can she buy?

_____

b How much does she have left over?

_____

155 A supporters' club hires six coaches to go to a tournament. Each coach has 53 seats and all the seats are occupied. How many supporters go to the tournament?

_____

156 A cinema seats 650 people when full. There are 26 rows, with the same number of seats in each row. How many seats are there in each row?

_____

157 The annual membership fee for a tennis club is $850 for men and $725 for women. How much will the membership cost for a year for a family of three men and two women?

_____

158 George has a wad of $100 bills that are numbered consecutively from 893712 to 893891. He is going to use all of them to buy a car. How much is the car?

_____

159 In a school with 672 students, it is estimated that each student will use 18 exercise books in the course of a school year. At the beginning of the school year there are 3394 books in stock. During the year the school receives two deliveries, one for 5500 books and another for 4550. Estimate the number of exercise books it should have in stock at the end of the year. Give your answer correct to the nearest 50.

_____

160 A truck proprietor owns three trucks. One truck can carry 25t, another can carry 15t and the third truck can carry 10t. How many journeys must each truck make to bring 3240t of hard core to a building site? Assume that each truck makes the same number of journeys.

_____

161 The product of three numbers is 4199. Two of the numbers are 13 and 17. Work out the other number.

_____

162 The Blackwood Building Company sends out invoices on the fifth of the month, to be paid by the second of the following month. Excluding the day on which the bill is sent, how many days are there in which to pay a bill sent out on:

a 5 September   _____

b 5 October?   _____

(There are 30 days in September and 31 in October.)

163 An assurance company organises a day out for its employees. Four different trips are available. When the final check is made the numbers are:

Trip A: 222   Trip B: 278

Trip C: 184   Trip D: 90

The company that supplies the coaches has a fleet of 47-seater coaches.

a How many coaches are needed altogether?

_____

b How many additional passengers can be taken on each trip if every seat is taken?

Trip A _____   Trip B _____

Trip C _____   Trip D _____

c The coach operator agreed that the total cost should be worked out by calculating the fares for each person who goes on a trip as follows:

Trip A: $30   Trip B: $35

Trip C: $25   Trip D: $28

How much did the assurance company have to pay for the four trips?

_____

d What extra income would the coach company have had if all the seats had been taken for all the trips?

164 A palette of building blocks consists of five layers, with each layer containing 27 blocks. How many palettes of blocks must be ordered if a particular building is expected to require 112 000 blocks?

165 There are 12 460 cans of peas in the stock room of a hypermarket. If 76 boxes, each containing 72 cans, are taken from the stock to display on the shelves, how many cans remain in stock?

166 In a school with 753 pupils, it is estimated that each pupil uses 16 exercise books in a year. At the beginning of the school year there are 2534 new books in stock, and during the year the school receives two deliveries, each of 5500 new books. How many books remain in stock at the end of the school year?

167 It costs $89 625 for an aeroplane to fly between two cities. If 264 passengers make the flight, travelling either first class or economy class, calculate the profit on the flight, given that there are 100 first class passengers who pay twice the economy fare of $504.

168 A catering pack contains 5000 grams of jam. If 12 grams of jam is used in each jam tart, how many tarts may be filled from five catering packs?

169 A length of road is 1600 metres long and is to be fenced off on both sides. A roll of fencing is 33 metres long.

a How many rolls are required?

b How much is left over?

170 Benjamin buys a car which should do 84 kilometres per gallon. He finds that it gives 76 kilometres per gallon. How much extra petrol will he need in a year when he travels 11 172 km?

171 Christoper Columbus is said the have discovered America in the fifteenth century.

a What are the first two digits of the year in which Columbus discovered America?

b The sum of the four digits in the year is 16. When the units digit is subtracted from the tens digit, the answer is 7. In what year did Columbus discover America?

2 Factors and indices

1 Write the following numbers as the product of two factors giving all possibilities:

a 24 _____

b 42 _____

c 105 _____

d 66 _____

e 114 _____

f 92 _____

2 Write the set of multiples of:

a 4 between 15 and 30 _____

b 7 between 20 and 40 _____

c 11 between 34 and 84 _____

d 6 between 35 and 55 _____

e 9 between 80 and 120 _____

f 8 between 20 and 60. _____

3 Write the factors of 84 that are odd.

_____

4 a Write all the factors of 72 that are even.

_____

b Which factors of 72 are odd?

_____

5 Find a number smaller than 36 that is a multiple of 6 and 9. _____

6 Find a number smaller than 50 that is a multiple of 4 and 14. _____

7 Which of these numbers are prime?

3, 6, 9, 11, 17, 19, 21, 23 _____

8 Find a number between 80 and 90 that is a multiple of 6 and 7. _____

9 Find the sum of all the whole numbers between 24 and 36 that are not multiples of 3.

_____

10 Find the sum of all the prime numbers between 20 and 40. _____

11 Which numbers in the following list are prime numbers?

27, 45, 53, 61, 71, 81 _____

12 Which numbers in the following list are not prime numbers?

29, 39, 49, 59, 69, 79 _____

13 Which numbers in the following list are not prime numbers?

27, 37, 47, 57, 67 _____

14 Are the following statements true or false?

a There are five prime numbers between 4 and 20. _____

b There are 10 prime numbers smaller than 30. _____

c The only even prime number is 2.

_____

15 Are the following statements true or false?

a There are exactly six prime numbers between 6 and 25. _____

b The next prime number after 29 is 37.

_____

c The prime number nearest to 40 is 37.

_____

16 Write the following products in index form:

a $2 \times 2 \times 2 \times 2$ _____

b $5 \times 5 \times 5$ _____

c $7 \times 7 \times 7 \times 7 \times 7 \times 7$ _____

d $3 \times 3 \times 3 \times 3$ _____

e $3 \times 3 \times 3 \times 3 \times 3$ _____

f $2 \times 2 \times 2 \times 2 \times 2 \times 2 \times 2$ _____

17 Find the value of:

a 2^4 _____

b 2^2 _____

c 10^5 _____

d 7^3 _____

e 3^3 _____

f 8^3 _____

18 Write these numbers as ordinary numbers:

a 4×10^3 _____

b $3 \times 10^2 + 4 \times 10^3$ _____

c 7×10^2 _____

d 5×10^4 _____

e $2 \times 10^3 + 3 \times 10^2$ _____

19 What number do you put in the box to make these correct?

a $\square^2 = 49$ _____

b $\square^3 = 125$ _____

c $\square^6 = 64$ _____

d $\square^3 = 343$ _____

e $\square^4 = 81$ _____

f $\square^5 = 32$ _____

20 Express these numbers in index form:

a 8 _____

b 27 _____

c 64 _____

d 729 _____

21 Find the value of a if:

a $5^a = 625$ _____

b $3^a = 729$ _____

c $4^a = 256$ _____

d $4^a = 64$ _____

e $7^a = 343$ _____

f $6^a = 216$ _____

22 Write these products in index form:

a $3 \times 3 \times 5 \times 5 \times 5$ _____

b $7 \times 3 \times 7 \times 3 \times 3$ _____

c $2 \times 3 \times 2 \times 3 \times 2 \times 5 \times 5 \times 3$

_____

d $3 \times 5 \times 3 \times 3 \times 5 \times 5 \times 7 \times 7 \times 5$

_____

e $2 \times 5 \times 2 \times 5 \times 2 \times 2 \times 2$

_____

23 Write these numbers as the product of their prime factors:

a 144 _____

b 675 _____

c 864 _____

d 252 _____

e 1144 _____

f 6075 _____

24 Write these numbers as the product of their prime factors:

a 216 _____

b 875 _____

c 1936 _____

d 1280 _____

e 41 503 _____

f 30 030 _____

25 a Is 342 divisible by 3? _____

b Is 2923 divisible by 5? _____

c Is 364 divisible by 7? _____

26 Look at the number 10 122.

a Is it divisible by 2? _____

b Is it divisible by 3? _____

c Is it divisible by 6? _____

27 An exercise has 50 questions. How many question numbers are exactly divisible by 7?

_____

28 State the HCF of:

a 12, 18 and 30 _____

b 25, 35 and 45 _____

c 39, 26 and 52 _____

d 42, 70 and 98 _____

e 35, 52 and 56 _____

f 42, 70 and 84 _____

g 6, 12 and 32 _____

29 Find the largest number of people who can share equally 72 CDs and 162 books.

_____

30 Find the HCF of:

a 45, 70 and 90 _____

b 21, 35 and 63 _____

c 8, 14 and 32 _____

31 Find the HCF of the following numbers, giving your answer as the product of its prime factors:

a 245 and 385 _____

b 325 and 720 _____

c 108, 162 and 270 _____

32 State the LCM of:

a 7 and 9 _____

b 3, 9 and 15 _____

c 8, 9 and 10 _____

33 Write, in index form, the LCM of:

a $2^2 \times 5$ and 2×5^3 _____

b $2^2 \times 3^2$ and 2×3^4 _____

c $2^2 \times 3 \times 5$ and $3^2 \times 5^3$ _____

34 Look at the numbers 31, 7, 21, 24, 13.

a Which of these numbers are:

i odd numbers _____

ii prime numbers _____

iii multiples of 3? _____

b For the largest of these numbers that is not prime, write all its factors.

_____

35 Which of the following numbers are square numbers?

a $3^2 \times 2^4$ _____

b $2^2 \times 3^3 \times 5$ _____

c $2^6 \times 3^2$ _____

36 What is the smallest whole number by which 12 must be multiplied to make it a multiple of 36?

_____

37 What is the smallest whole number by which 3^3 must be multiplied to make it a square number?

_____

38 Find the least sum of money into which 12c, 24c and 42c will divide exactly.

_____

39 Two toy cars go round a circular track. One car takes three seconds for a complete circuit and the other car takes five seconds. If they start together, how long will it be before they are side by side again?

40 Rectangular tiles measure 15 cm by 9 cm. What is the length of the smallest square area that can be covered with these tiles?

41 A rectangular–shaped patio measures 550 cm by 330 cm. What are the dimensions of the largest square stone that can be used to pave the area without cutting?

42 Jenny, Steve and Molly go to Mrs Layne for music lessons. Jenny goes every fourth day, Steve every eighth day and Molly every sixth day. They all go for a lesson on Tuesday 1 June. On what date and day of the week will they next all have a lesson on the same day?

43 Find the largest number of children who can share equally 126 oranges and 147 bananas.

44 An exercise has 31 questions. How many questions:

a have even numbers

b have numbers that are a multiple of 5?

45 Find the largest number of children that can share equally 54 pencils and 24 pens.

46 Find the smallest number of dollars that can be divided exactly into equal amounts of $3 or $6 or $8.

47 a Is 564 divisible by 3?

b State the LCM of 4, 8 and 20.

c State the HCF of 21, 42 and 63.

48 a Is 10 354 divisible by 6?

b State the LCM of 15, 20 and 25.

c State the HCF of 52, 39 and 26.

49 a Is 1364 divisible by 5?

b State the LCM of 4, 8 and 20.

c Find the HCF of 432 and 768.

50 a Is 26 070 divisible by 15?

b State the LCM of 44, 121 and 66.

c State the HCF of 245 and 385.

3   Sets

1 Describe in words a set which includes the given members.

   a {January, February, March}

   _____

   b {France, Germany, Italy}

   _____

   c {II, IV, VI, VIII}

   _____

   d {a, b, c, d, e, f}

   _____

   e {Mandeville, Ocho Rios, Savanna-la-Mar, Spanish Town}

   _____

2 Describe in words a set which includes the given members:

   a {January, June, July}

   _____

   b {alsatian, poodle, schipperke}

   _____

   c {Antigua, Barbuda, Dominica}

   _____

   d {Bridgetown, Speightstown, Oistins}

   _____

3 Describe a set which includes the given members and state another member of it:

   a {4, 8, 12, 16, 24}

   _____

   b {25, 9, 16, 1, 49}

   _____

   c {Paris, London, Rome}

   _____

   d {Nile, Amazon, Mississippi}

   _____

   e {Antigua, St Lucia, Jamaica}

   _____

4 Describe a set which includes the given members and state another member of it:

   a {6, 9, 18, 36}

   _____

   b {Brasilia, Lima, Santiago}

   _____

   c {California, Nebraska, Wyoming}

   _____

   d {Rhine, Thames, Seine}

   _____

5 List the members in each of these sets:

   a {prime numbers between 4 and 24}

   _____

   b {the letters used in the word Caribbean}

   _____

   c {the last six letters of the alphabet}

d {whole numbers greater than 12 but less than 25}

_____

e {whole numbers between 3 and 25 that are exactly divisible by both 3 and 4}

_____

6 Write these statements in set notation:

a Banana is a member of the set of fruit.

_____

b Mathematics is a member of the set of school subjects.

_____

c February is a member of the set of months of the year.

_____

d Garry Sobers is a member of the set of famous cricketers.

_____

e Lionel Messi is a member of the set of famous football players.

_____

7 Write these statements in set notation:

a Panda is not a member of the set of fruit.

_____

b France is not a member of the set of Caribbean countries.

_____

c New York is not a member of the set of capital cities.

_____

d Sandal is not a member of the set of furniture.

_____

e Boeing is not a member of the set of motorcar manufacturers.

_____

8 Write these statements in set notation:

a China is not a member of the set of European countries.

_____

b Rolls Royce is a member of the set of motorcar manufacturers.

_____

c Britain is not a member of the set of Caribbean countries.

_____

d A television set is not a member of the set of colours.

_____

e A set square is a member of the set of carpenters' tools.

_____

9 Using the correct notation write:

a two members that belong to

{rivers of the world}

_____

b two members that do not belong to

{rivers of the world}

_____

10 Using the correct notation, write two members that belong to the set of:

a clothes

_____

b girls' names

_____

c kitchen utensils

_____

d trees

_____

e building materials.

_____

11 Write the following sentences in set notation:

a Chair is not a member of the set of cars.

_____

b Bee is a member of the set of living things.

_____

c Aeroplane is not a member of the set of boys' names.

_____

d Curtain is not a member of the set of floor coverings.

_____

e Argentina is a member of the set of South American countries.

_____

12 Write the following sentences in set notation:

a Rabbit is not a member of the set of dogs.

_____

b Equador is a member of the set of South American countries.

_____

c Mount Everest is not a member of the set of rivers of the world.

_____

d Judaism is a member of the set of the religions of the world.

_____

e Mathematics is a member of the set of subjects studied at school.

_____

13 Which of the following sets are equal? Write the letters of your answers on the answer line below.

_____

a A = {prime numbers between 10 and 20}
   B = {11, 13, 17, 19}

b X = {consonants}
   Y = {b, o, z, f, m, u, z}

c S = {all oceans}
   T = {Pacific, Atlantic, Indian}

d E = {letters in the word 'metal'}
   F = {l, a, m, t, e}

14 Which of the following sets are equivalent? Write the letters of your answers on the answer line below.

_____

a A = {prime numbers between 10 and 20}
   B = {20, 25, 31, 37}

b C = {mammals}
   D = {dog, cat, fox, wolf}

c P = {a, b, c, d, e}
   Q = {v, w, x, y, z}

d K = {number of students in your class}
   L = {number of people in your family}

15 Write the meaning of the following:

a cocoa $\in$ {beverages}

_____

b trapeziums $\notin$ {rectangles}

_____

c chemistry $\in$ {school subjects}

_____

d zebra $\notin$ {girls' names}

_____

16 Which of these are empty sets?

a {dogs with three legs} _____

b {cats with three ears} _____

c {men with a mass more than 200 kg}

_____

d {cars with 9 wheels} _____

17 Which of these are empty sets?

a {women with three eyes} _____

b {mice with gills} _____

c {cars with three wheels} _____

d {fish that cannot swim} _____

e {spiders with eight legs} _____

18 Suggest a suitable universal set for:

a {consonants}

_____

b {salamanders}

_____

c {subjects you are studying in school}

_____

19 Suggest a suitable universal set for:

a {dining furniture}

_____

b {vowels}

_____

c {china cups}

_____

d {elephants}

_____

e {whales}

_____

20 If $A = \{p, q, r, s\}$ write all the subsets that have:

a two members _____

b three members. _____

21 If $A = \{a, b, c, d\}$ write all the subsets that have:

a three members _____

b two members _____

c one member. _____

22 If $B = \{5, 6, 7, \ldots 15\}$ which of the following sets are subsets of B?

a {positive odd numbers less than 16}

_____

b {odd numbers between 4 and 16}

_____

c {prime numbers between 4 and 15}

_____

23 If $P = \{3, 4, 5, \ldots 20\}$ which of the following sets are subsets of P?

   a {odd numbers bigger than 8 but smaller than 20}

_____

   b {multiples of 5 less than 20}

_____

   c {prime numbers between 4 and 20}

_____

24 Write two subsets, each with at least two members, for each of the following universal sets:

   a {Caribbean countries}

_____

   b {American states}

_____

   c {rivers of the world}

_____

   d {cities in the USA}

_____

25 Write two subsets, each with at least two members, for each of the following universal sets:

   a {planets}

_____

   b {European cities}

_____

   c {British cities}

_____

   d {mountains of the world}

_____

26 Find the union of the following pairs of sets:

   a $A = \{2, 5, 7, 8\}$, $B = \{1, 2, 5, 6, 8, 9\}$

_____

   b $P = \{p, q, r\}$, $Q = \{r, s, t, u\}$

_____

   c $D = $ {letters in the word 'programme'}, $E = $ {letters in the word 'metre'}

_____

   d $J = $ {whole numbers that divide exactly into 15}, $K = $ {whole numbers that divide exactly into 12}

_____

27 Find the union of the following pairs of sets:

   a $A = $ {letters in the word PIGEON}, $B = $ {letters in the word CHICKEN}

_____

   b $P = \{p, q, r, s\}$, $Q = \{r, s, t, u, v\}$

_____

   c $R = \{3, 6, 9, 12, 15\}$, $S = \{6, 8, 10, 12, 16\}$

_____

   d $D = $ {even numbers less than 15}, $E = $ {multiples of 3 less than 20}

_____

28 Draw suitable Venn diagrams to show the unions of the following pairs of sets:

   a $A = \{d, e, f, g\}$, $B = \{g, h, i, j\}$

b $P = \{6, 9, 12, 15, 18\}$, $Q = \{6, 10, 14, 18, 22\}$

c $C = \{$prime numbers less than 20$\}$,
$D = \{$odd numbers larger than 6 but smaller than 20$\}$

c $R = \{$letters in the word 'Kingston'$\}$,
$S = \{$letters in the word 'Bridgetown'$\}$

d $P = \{9, 10, 11, 13, 16, 18\}$,
$Q = \{8, 10, 13, 14, 15, 16\}$

d $V = \{$odd numbers less than 14$\}$,
$W = \{$multiples of 3 less than 20$\}$

30 Draw suitable Venn diagrams to show the unions of the following pairs of sets:

a $A = \{$letter in the word PHILOSOPHY$\}$,
$B = \{$letters in the word IDEOLOGY$\}$

29 Draw suitable Venn diagrams to show the unions of the following pairs of sets:

a $X = \{a, b, c, d, e\}$, $Y = \{a, c, e, g, i\}$

b $C = \{$multiples of 3 less than 25$\}$,
$D = \{$multiples of 4 less than 25$\}$

b $A = \{$letters in the word WASHINGTON$\}$,
$B = \{$letters in the words NEW YORK$\}$

c $P = \{$letters in the word SILHOUETTE$\}$,
$Q = \{$letters in the word MINSTREL$\}$

d X = {prime numbers bigger than 20 but smaller than 40},

Y = {odd numbers bigger than 24 but smaller than 38}

33 Draw suitable Venn diagrams to show the intersections of the following pairs of sets:

a A = {3, 6, 9, 12, 15},
B = {4, 6, 8, 10, 12}

31 Find the intersection of the following pairs of sets:

a E = {m, n, p, q, r}, F = {q, r, s, t, u}

_____

b X = {prime numbers greater than 10 but smaller than 20}, Y = {factors of 24}

_____

b C = {whole numbers less than 20},
D = {prime numbers less than 20}

c T = {letters in the word 'Barbados'},
U = {letters in the word 'Tobago'}

_____

c E = {letters in the word 'ancestor'},
F = {letters in the word 'descendant'}

d G = {Elsie, George, Penny, Fleur},
H = {Peter, Clive, Elsie, Joe}

_____

34 Draw suitable Venn diagrams to show the intersections of the following pairs of sets:

32 Find the intersection of the following pairs of sets:

a A = {l, m, n, p, q}, B = {p, q, r, s, t}

_____

a A = {2, 4, 9, 14, 15},
B = {3, 6, 9, 12, 16}

b C = {letters in the word APPENDIX},
D = {letters in the word PREFIXES}

_____

b X = {15, 18, 21, 24, 27},
Y = {3,6,9,12,16}

c E = {whole numbers smaller than 30 but larger than 10},

F = {prime numbers smaller than 25}

_____

c P = {letters in the word PERFECT},
Q = {letters in the word EXEMPLARY}

39 Given that X = {factors of 36} and
Y = {factors of 45} list all the members of:

a $X \cap Y$

_____

b $X \cup Y$

_____

35 Given A = {factors of 30} and
B = {factors of 42}, list the members of:

a $A \cup B$

_____

b $A \cap B$

_____

40

Use this Venn diagram to list all the
members of:

a A _____

b B _____

c $A \cup B$ _____

d $A \cap B$ _____

36

List the members of:

a A _____

b B _____

c $A \cup B$ _____

d $A \cap B$ _____

37 Set X has nine members and set Y has seven
members. State:

a the largest possible number of members

in set $X \cap Y$ _____

b the smallest possible number of members

in set $X \cup Y$. _____

38 S = {students wearing spectacles},
F = {pupils with fair hair}

a Describe $S \cap F$

_____

b Draw a Venn diagram and shade $S \cap F$

41 Set P has five members and set Q has eight
members, all of which are different.

a The largest number of members in $P \cap Q$ is

_____

b The smallest number of members in

$P \cup Q$ is _____

42 C = {boys wearing white shirts}
D = {boys with dark hair}

a Describe $C \cap D$

_____

b Draw a Venn diagram and shade $C \cap D$

Use this diagram for questions **1** to **3**. Select the letter that gives the correct answer.

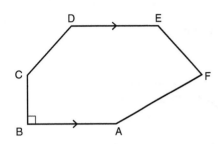

1 AB is called a:

    A vertex   **B** straight line

    C line segment   **D** ray.

2 The name given to this shape is a:

    A parallelogram   **B** pentagon

    C hexagon   **D** none of these.

3 The line segments AB and ED are:

    A perpendicular   **B** parallel

    C equal in length   **D** none of these.

For each shape in questions **4** to **9** write:

    a how many sides it has

    b how many angles there are inside the shape

    c the name of the shape.

4

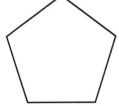

a _____

b _____

c _____

5

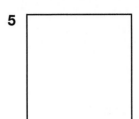

a _____

b _____

c _____

6

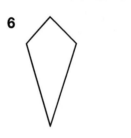

a _____

b _____

c _____

7

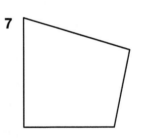

a _____

b _____

c _____

8

a _____

b _____

c _____

9

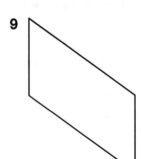

a _____

b _____

c _____

10 ABCD is a square of side 4 cm.

Mark K, L, M, N the midpoints of the sides AB, BC, CD and DA respectively.

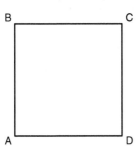

a Join KM. What is its length? _____

b Join LN. What is its length? _____

Join KLMNK in order.

c What name do we give to this shape?

_____

d Join AC. Measure and record its length.

_____

e Join BD. Measure and record its length.

_____

f How do your answers to parts **d** and **e**

compare? _____

11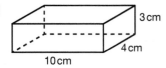

a What name do we give to this solid?

_____

b How many edges does it have?

_____

c How many vertices does it have?

_____

d What is the total length of all the longest

edges? _____

e What is the total length of all the shortest

edges? _____

f How many faces does this solid have?

_____

g How many faces measure 10 cm by 3 cm?

_____

h What are the measurements of the smallest

faces? _____

i What are the measurements of the largest

faces? _____

j What name do we give to the shape of

each of the faces? _____

k What is the total length of all the edges?

_____

12 This solid is called a tetrahedron.
All its edges are the same length.

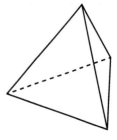

a How many edges does it have? _____

b How many vertices does it have? _____

c What name is given to the shape of each

face? _____

d How many faces are there? _____

All the edges are the same length.

e What special name is given to this
tetrahedron?

_____

13 This solid is a pyramid with a square base.
The broken lines show hidden edges.
It stands on a flat surface.
All the edges are the same length.

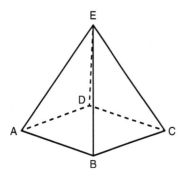

a How many edges does it have?

_____

b How many vertices does it have?

_____

c What name is given to the shape of each

sloping face? _____

d How many faces are there?

_____

e How many edges can you see in the

diagram? _____

f Where do you find very large ancient

buildings with this shape? _____

14 a What name is given to a solid with six
identical square faces?

_____

b How many edges does it have?

_____

c How many vertices does it have?

_____

15 What name is given to each of the shapes
described below?

a A polygon with five sides.

_____

b A plane figure bounded by four straight line
segments.

_____

c A quadrilateral with both pairs of opposite
sides equal and parallel.

_____

16 Which of these shapes will tessellate? Where
they will, draw sketches to show how they fit
together.

a

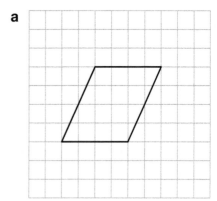

_____

b

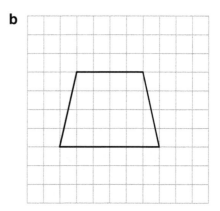

_____

c

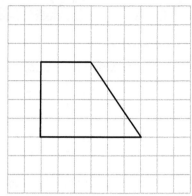

e

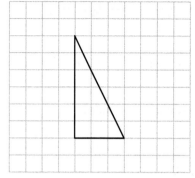

d

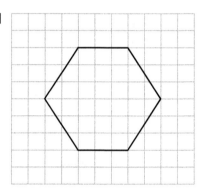

f

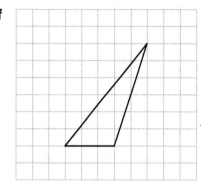

5 Fractions: addition and subtraction

1 Express the first quantity as a fraction of the second:

a 45 seconds; 3 minutes

_____

b 60c; $2

_____

c 50 minutes; 2 hours

_____

d 5 days; the number of days in the month of June.

_____

2 Fill in the missing numbers to make equivalent fractions:

a $\dfrac{7}{10} = \dfrac{}{50}$ **b** $\dfrac{4}{9} = \dfrac{}{36}$

c $\dfrac{4}{7} = \dfrac{12}{}$ **d** $\dfrac{2}{33} = \dfrac{}{99}$

e $\dfrac{5}{8} = \dfrac{35}{}$

3 Write each fraction as an equivalent fraction with denominator 36:

a $\dfrac{3}{4}$ _____   **b** $\dfrac{7}{9}$ _____

c $\dfrac{11}{12}$ _____   **d** $\dfrac{11}{18}$ _____

4 Which fraction is the larger?

a $\dfrac{3}{5}$ or $\dfrac{4}{7}$ _____

b $\dfrac{2}{11}$ or $\dfrac{3}{20}$ _____

c $\dfrac{5}{9}$ or $\dfrac{5}{8}$ _____

5 Put either > or < between the fractions:

a $\dfrac{3}{11}$ $\dfrac{2}{7}$ **b** $\dfrac{9}{11}$ $\dfrac{3}{4}$

c $\dfrac{3}{8}$ $\dfrac{5}{12}$ **d** $\dfrac{5}{9}$ $\dfrac{6}{11}$

6 Arrange the following fractions in ascending order:

a $\dfrac{13}{24}, \dfrac{2}{3}, \dfrac{7}{12}, \dfrac{5}{6}, \dfrac{5}{8}$ _____

b $\dfrac{2}{9}, \dfrac{7}{18}, \dfrac{1}{3}, \dfrac{5}{6}, \dfrac{4}{9}$ _____

c $\dfrac{3}{10}, \dfrac{2}{5}, \dfrac{7}{25}, \dfrac{13}{50}, \dfrac{3}{5}$ _____

d $\dfrac{3}{5}, \dfrac{7}{9}, \dfrac{11}{12}, \dfrac{3}{4}$ _____

7 Simplify the following fractions:

a $\dfrac{27}{36}$ _____   **b** $\dfrac{24}{42}$ _____

c $\dfrac{55}{121}$ _____   **d** $\dfrac{36}{84}$ _____

e $\dfrac{63}{81}$ _____   **f** $\dfrac{36}{60}$ _____

g $\dfrac{75}{125}$ _____   **h** $\dfrac{48}{400}$ _____

8 Add the fractions, simplifying the answers where you can:

a $\dfrac{7}{15} + \dfrac{8}{15}$ _____

b $\dfrac{8}{21} + \dfrac{4}{21}$ _____

c $\dfrac{9}{30} + \dfrac{7}{30}$ _____

d $\dfrac{3}{10} + \dfrac{7}{10}$ _____

e $\dfrac{11}{30} + \dfrac{19}{30}$ _____

f $\dfrac{7}{12} + \dfrac{5}{12} + \dfrac{1}{12}$ _____

9 Add the fractions, simplifying the answers where you can:

a $\dfrac{7}{24} + \dfrac{1}{24} + \dfrac{11}{24} + \dfrac{2}{24}$ _____

b $\dfrac{3}{13} + \dfrac{2}{13} + \dfrac{6}{13} + \dfrac{1}{13}$ _____

c $\dfrac{3}{77} + \dfrac{12}{77} + \dfrac{13}{77} + \dfrac{5}{77}$ _____

10 Find:

a $\dfrac{2}{5} + \dfrac{1}{6}$ _____

b $\dfrac{3}{10} + \dfrac{2}{3}$ _____

c $\dfrac{1}{6} + \dfrac{2}{7}$ _____

d $\dfrac{7}{16} + \dfrac{3}{8}$ _____

e $\dfrac{1}{4} + \dfrac{11}{16}$ _____

f $\dfrac{3}{11} + \dfrac{5}{9}$ _____

11 Add the fractions, simplifying the answers where you can:

a $\dfrac{2}{15} + \dfrac{7}{30}$ _____

b $\dfrac{2}{11} + \dfrac{5}{9}$ _____

c $\dfrac{4}{15} + \dfrac{1}{5} + \dfrac{3}{10}$ _____

d $\dfrac{1}{12} + \dfrac{1}{4} + \dfrac{1}{8}$ _____

e $\dfrac{4}{15} + \dfrac{7}{10} + \dfrac{3}{5}$ _____

f $\dfrac{1}{2} + \dfrac{1}{3} + \dfrac{1}{4}$ _____

12 Find, and simplify where you can:

a $\dfrac{9}{13} - \dfrac{4}{13}$ _____

b $\dfrac{11}{16} - \dfrac{5}{16}$ _____

c $\dfrac{21}{100} - \dfrac{6}{100}$ _____

d $\dfrac{17}{18} - \dfrac{5}{6}$ _____

e $\dfrac{19}{32} - \dfrac{3}{8}$ _____

f $\dfrac{7}{8} - \dfrac{3}{4}$ _____

13 Find, and simplify where you can:

a $\dfrac{11}{12} - \dfrac{5}{8} + \dfrac{1}{4}$ _____

b $\dfrac{5}{6} + \dfrac{2}{9} - \dfrac{2}{3}$ _____

c $\dfrac{1}{2} + \dfrac{3}{10} - \dfrac{57}{100}$ _____

d $\dfrac{4}{7} + \dfrac{10}{21} - \dfrac{3}{14}$ _____

e $\dfrac{4}{9} + \dfrac{2}{3} - \dfrac{11}{12}$ _____

f $\dfrac{17}{30} - \dfrac{2}{5} + \dfrac{1}{16}$ _____

14 Express as mixed or whole numbers:

a $\dfrac{40}{12}$ _____   **b** $\dfrac{12}{8}$ _____

c $\dfrac{44}{3}$ _____   **d** $\dfrac{60}{15}$ _____

e $\dfrac{70}{13}$ _____   **f** $\dfrac{73}{21}$ _____

15 Change these improper fractions to mixed numbers:

a $\dfrac{43}{9}$ _____   **b** $\dfrac{59}{7}$ _____

c $\dfrac{96}{11}$ _____

d $\dfrac{45}{8}$ _____

e $\dfrac{29}{4}$ _____

f $\dfrac{520}{13}$ _____

16 Change these mixed numbers to improper fractions:

a $5\frac{1}{4}$ _____

b $8\frac{3}{5}$ _____

c $12\frac{3}{7}$ _____

d $8\frac{2}{5}$ _____

e $7\frac{3}{4}$ _____

f $16\frac{1}{5}$ _____

17 Calculate the following divisions, giving your answers as mixed numbers:

a $46 \div 11$ _____

b $31 \div 14$ _____

c $76 \div 12$ _____

d $17 \div 8$ _____

e $34 \div 5$ _____

f $100 \div 7$ _____

18 Find:

a $5\frac{1}{3}+2\frac{1}{6}$ _____

b $3\frac{11}{12}+1\frac{1}{4}$ _____

c $2\frac{1}{2}+7\frac{9}{16}$ _____

d $1\frac{1}{2}+\frac{3}{4}$ _____

e $4\frac{3}{4}+1\frac{7}{8}$ _____

f $7\frac{5}{8}+2\frac{1}{2}$ _____

19 Find:

a $5\frac{1}{3}+3\frac{3}{4}+7\frac{2}{5}$ _____

b $7\frac{3}{10}+2\frac{5}{8}+3\frac{1}{2}$ _____

c $4\frac{5}{14}+2\frac{4}{9}+3\frac{2}{7}$ _____

d $4\frac{7}{8}+5\frac{3}{4}+7\frac{1}{2}$ _____

e $1\frac{3}{5}+\frac{2}{5}+2\frac{1}{10}$ _____

f $5\frac{3}{10}+1\frac{5}{8}+2\frac{1}{4}$ _____

20 Find:

a $\dfrac{3}{4}-\dfrac{2}{3}$ _____

b $\dfrac{3}{5}-\dfrac{7}{20}$ _____

c $\dfrac{3}{4}-\dfrac{1}{16}-\dfrac{2}{5}$ _____

d $\dfrac{4}{5}-\dfrac{5}{7}$ _____

e $\dfrac{2}{3}-\dfrac{1}{4}-\dfrac{1}{6}$ _____

f $\dfrac{5}{6}-\dfrac{5}{12}-\dfrac{1}{16}$ _____

21 Find:

a $9\frac{3}{4}-7\frac{5}{8}$ _____

b $5\frac{7}{8}-4\frac{3}{5}$ _____

c $12\frac{11}{16}-7\frac{1}{2}$ _____

d $9\frac{7}{12}-3\frac{1}{3}$ _____

e $5\frac{3}{4}-2\frac{3}{8}$ _____

22 Find:

a $7\frac{1}{2}-3\frac{2}{3}$ _____

b $6\frac{1}{4}-1\frac{5}{8}$ _____

c $10\frac{3}{8}-7\frac{3}{4}$ _____

d $7\frac{1}{2}-1\frac{1}{3}$ _____

e $10\frac{3}{4}-7\frac{5}{8}$ _____

23 Find:

a $5\frac{2}{5}+4\frac{5}{6}-6\frac{3}{4}$ _____

b $4\frac{7}{12}-3\frac{5}{8}+1\frac{2}{3}$ _____

c $12\frac{6}{7} - 5\frac{1}{3} - 1\frac{1}{4}$ _____

d $4\frac{7}{12} - 3\frac{5}{8} + 1\frac{2}{3}$ _____

e $12\frac{1}{4} - 7\frac{5}{6} + 4\frac{11}{12}$ _____

24 What must be added to $\frac{1}{2} + \frac{1}{4} + \frac{1}{8}$ to make 1?

_____

25 What must be added to $\frac{1}{3} + \frac{1}{4} + \frac{1}{5}$ to make 1?

_____

26 How much smaller than 3 is $\frac{2}{3} + \frac{5}{6} + \frac{1}{4}$?

_____

27 How much larger than 2 is $\frac{2}{3} + \frac{5}{6} + \frac{3}{4}$?

_____

28 How much smaller than 2 is $\frac{2}{3} + \frac{5}{6} + \frac{1}{4}$?

_____

29 Which is smaller and by how much?

$\dfrac{5}{7} - \dfrac{2}{3} + \dfrac{1}{6}$ or $\dfrac{3}{4} - \dfrac{2}{7} - \dfrac{5}{28}$

_____

30 Which is smaller and by how much?

$\dfrac{7}{8} + \dfrac{1}{4} - \dfrac{2}{3}$ or $\dfrac{5}{8} - \dfrac{1}{2} + \dfrac{7}{12}$

_____

31 Which is larger and by how much?

$\dfrac{1}{6} + \dfrac{1}{8} - \dfrac{1}{4}$ or $\dfrac{1}{3} - \dfrac{2}{9} + \dfrac{1}{6}$

_____

32 A box contains oranges but $\frac{3}{8}$ of them are found to be bad. What fraction of the oranges are satisfactory?

_____

33 A petrol storage tank is $\frac{3}{4}$ full. After a quantity of petrol is drawn off, the tank is $\frac{3}{5}$ full. What fraction of a full tank is drawn off?

_____

34 In a history textbook, $\frac{2}{5}$ of it deals with the eighteenth century, $\frac{3}{7}$ with the nineteenth century and the remainder with the twentieth century. What fraction of the book is devoted to the twentieth century?

_____

35 Eddy has a 2 litre tin of paint which is two-thirds full. After he has given a door one coat of paint the tin is seven-twelfths full. What fraction of the tin was needed to paint the door?

_____

36 An airline allows each passenger 22 kg of luggage. Maxine has one case of mass $9\frac{5}{6}$ kg and another of mass $7\frac{4}{9}$ kg. How many kilograms is she under the limit?

_____

37 In a class of students, half of them come by bus, two-fifths come by car and the remainder walk.

a What fraction of the students walk to school?

_____

b What fraction do not come by car?

_____

38 Of the 525 pupils at Weston School, $\frac{1}{3}$ travel by bus, $\frac{1}{5}$ travel by car and the rest cycle.

a What fraction of the pupils cycle to school?

_____

b How many pupils cycle to school?

_____

39 Year 10 pupils have to choose one subject out of chemistry, physics, biology and geography. If $\frac{1}{5}$ choose chemistry, $\frac{1}{6}$ physics, 21 choose biology and $\frac{2}{5}$ choose geography. How many pupils choose:

a chemistry _____

b geography _____

c physics? _____

40 Velma baked a cake. She gave one-sixth of it to Kevin and half of the remainder to Marcia. What fraction of the cake remains?

_____

41 A sum of money was divided between four girls. The first girl received one-third of it, the second girl two-fifths and the third girl one-sixth. What fraction did the fourth girl receive?

_____

6 Fractions: multiplication and division

1 Find:

a $\dfrac{5}{8} \times \dfrac{3}{10}$ _____

b $\dfrac{20}{21} \times \dfrac{7}{4}$ _____

c $\dfrac{7}{12} \times \dfrac{9}{28} \times \dfrac{4}{5}$ _____

2 Find:

a $\dfrac{2}{3} \times \dfrac{5}{9}$ _____

b $\dfrac{7}{12} \times \dfrac{3}{5}$ _____

c $\dfrac{4}{7} \times \dfrac{7}{4}$ _____

3 Find:

a $4\frac{1}{2} \times \dfrac{4}{9}$ _____

b $5\frac{1}{3} \times 1\frac{3}{8}$ _____

c $1\frac{2}{5} \times 2\frac{1}{2}$ _____

4 Find:

a $7\frac{3}{5} \times \dfrac{5}{19}$ _____

b $4\frac{1}{2} \times \dfrac{4}{9}$ _____

c $\dfrac{4}{7} \times 4\frac{3}{8}$ _____

5 Find:

a $2\frac{5}{8} \times \dfrac{3}{7} \times 2\frac{2}{5}$ _____

b $3\frac{1}{6} \times 1\frac{5}{7} \times 5\frac{1}{4}$ _____

c $3\frac{3}{7} \times 1\frac{5}{9} \times 2\frac{1}{8}$ _____

6 Find:

a $\dfrac{2}{17} \times 3\frac{1}{8} \times 1\frac{7}{10}$ _____

b $4\frac{1}{2} \times 3\frac{2}{3} \times 1\frac{1}{11}$ _____

c $1\frac{2}{5} \times 2\frac{1}{4} \times 4\frac{1}{3}$ _____

7 Find:

a $2\frac{1}{9} \times 18$ _____

b $3\frac{2}{7} \times 21$ _____

c $4 \times 3\frac{3}{8}$ _____

8 Find:

a $12 \times 3\frac{2}{3}$ _____

b $2\frac{1}{4} \times 8$ _____

c $5\frac{1}{7} \times 14$ _____

9 Find:

a $\dfrac{1}{5}$ of 45 _____

b $\dfrac{5}{8}$ of 40 _____

c $\dfrac{3}{7}$ of 77 _____

d $\dfrac{7}{12}$ of 84 _____

10 Find:

a $\dfrac{1}{6}$ of 36 _____

b $\dfrac{3}{5}$ of 25 _____

c $\dfrac{5}{7}$ of 49 _____

d $\dfrac{5}{8}$ of 48 _____

11 Find:

a $\dfrac{5}{7}$ of 63 litres _____

b $\dfrac{4}{9}$ of 108 metres _____

c $\dfrac{3}{11}$ of 99 days _____

d $\dfrac{7}{8}$ of $42 _____

12 Find:

a $\dfrac{4}{5}$ of 65 centimetres _____

b $\dfrac{5}{11}$ of 198 days _____

c $\dfrac{3}{8}$ of $96 _____

d $\dfrac{2}{9}$ of 45 litres _____

13 a How many $\frac{1}{3}$s are there in 4? _____

b How many $\frac{3}{5}$s are there in 12? _____

c How many $\frac{2}{5}$s are there in 8? _____

14 a How many $\frac{1}{4}$s are there in 3? _____

b How many $\frac{2}{3}$s are there in 8? _____

c How many $\frac{3}{4}$s are there in 12? _____

15 Find:

a $12 \div \dfrac{4}{5}$ _____

b $27 \div \dfrac{9}{11}$ _____

c $\dfrac{14}{19} \div \dfrac{7}{2}$ _____

d $\dfrac{28}{27} \div \dfrac{4}{9}$ _____

16 Find:

a $\dfrac{1}{3} \div 3$ _____

b $\dfrac{1}{4} \div \dfrac{1}{2}$ _____

c $1 \div \dfrac{9}{10}$ _____

d $\dfrac{9}{16} \div \dfrac{3}{4}$ _____

17 Find:

a $4\frac{1}{2} \div 1\frac{1}{2}$ _____

b $6\frac{2}{5} \div 9\frac{3}{5}$ _____

c $4\frac{1}{3} \div 9\frac{3}{4}$ _____

d $5\frac{1}{3} \div 1\frac{1}{7}$ _____

18 Find:

a $1\frac{1}{2} \div \frac{2}{3}$ _____

b $3\frac{3}{5} \div 2\frac{7}{10}$ _____

c $1\frac{1}{2} \div 1\frac{1}{5}$ _____

d $4\frac{2}{5} \div 5\frac{1}{2}$ _____

19 Divide:

a $4\frac{2}{5}$ by $5\frac{1}{2}$ _____

b $2\frac{1}{3}$ by $1\frac{5}{9}$ _____

c $4\frac{1}{7}$ by $2\frac{5}{12}$ _____

20 Find:

a $5\frac{1}{3} \times 2\frac{5}{8} \div 4\frac{2}{3}$ _____

b $4\frac{2}{3} \div \frac{5}{9} \times 2\frac{1}{2}$ _____

c $3\frac{3}{7} \div 11\frac{2}{3} \times 8\frac{1}{6}$ _____

d $2\frac{1}{2} \div \frac{5}{9} \times 4\frac{2}{3}$ _____

21 Find $\left(5\frac{5}{8} \times \frac{3}{14}\right) \div \left(\frac{3}{4} + \frac{3}{14}\right)$

_____

22 Find $\left(5\frac{1}{5} \times 4\frac{1}{4}\right) \div \left(5\frac{1}{5} + 4\frac{1}{4}\right)$

_____

23 Calculate:

a $\frac{3}{8} + \frac{3}{4} \div \frac{1}{2}$ _____

b $\frac{4}{9} \div \left(\frac{5}{6} - \frac{2}{3}\right)$ _____

c $\frac{3}{4} + \left(\frac{5}{7} \div \frac{3}{4}\right) \times 4\frac{1}{5}$ _____

d $\frac{5}{12} - \frac{7}{20} \times \left(\frac{4}{7} - \frac{1}{3}\right)$ _____

24 Find:

a $1\frac{2}{5} \times \left(\frac{2}{3} - \frac{1}{4}\right) + \frac{1}{4}$ _____

b $1\frac{17}{18} \div 1\frac{4}{5} \times 2\frac{7}{10}$ _____

c $3\frac{3}{7} \times 8\frac{1}{6} \div 11\frac{2}{3}$ _____

25 Find:

a $6\frac{1}{2} - \frac{3}{4} - 3\frac{1}{4}$ _____

b $1\frac{1}{2} + 5\frac{1}{8} - 5\frac{3}{4}$ _____

c $4\frac{1}{2} - 2\frac{1}{3} \times 1\frac{1}{2}$ _____

d $1\frac{4}{5} \div \frac{3}{4} \times 2\frac{1}{7}$ _____

26 Find:

a $3\frac{2}{3} \div 1\frac{5}{9} \div 1\frac{5}{28}$ _____

b $\left(2\frac{1}{2} - 1\frac{3}{8}\right) \div \frac{3}{4}$ _____

c $\frac{9}{10} \div \frac{3}{8} \div 3\frac{1}{5}$ _____

27 How many $4\frac{1}{2}$ cm lengths of wire can be cut from a coil of wire that is 90 cm long?

_____

28 How many bottles of squash, each holding $\frac{7}{10}$ litre, can Sally fill from a cask holding $10\frac{1}{2}$ litres?

_____

29 In a local election there were two candidates. Denroy Perry got $\frac{5}{12}$ of the votes and Lorna LaPlace got $\frac{1}{3}$ of the votes. There were 3000 people who were entitled to vote did not do so.

a What fraction of the electorate:

i voted _____

ii did not vote? _____

b How large is the electorate?

_____

c How many votes did Lorna LaPlace get?

_____

30 An exercise has 50 questions. How many question numbers are exactly divisible by 7?

_____

31 An exercise has 80 questions. How many question numbers are exactly divisible by 9?

_____

32 My school is divided into lower school, middle school and upper school. One quarter of the students are in upper school, $\frac{2}{5}$ in middle school and 301 in lower school.

a What fraction of the students are in lower school?

_____

b How many students are there in the school?

_____

33 How many lengths of wire, each $4\frac{1}{2}$ cm long, can be cut from a coil of wire that is 90 cm long?

_____

34 A doctor estimates that it takes him $5\frac{1}{2}$ minutes to see a patient in his surgery.

a How many patients does he expect to see in his morning surgery which lasts $1\frac{3}{4}$ hours?

_____

b Evening surgery is timetabled to last $1\frac{1}{4}$ hours. Fifteen patients wait to see him. Will he be able to see all of them in $1\frac{1}{4}$ hours?

_____

35 If it takes $3\frac{3}{4}$ minutes to read 50 lines of a novel how long does it take to read:

a one line _____

b 350 lines. _____

36 A fuel storage tank is three-quarters full. After 75 litres have been drawn off it is three-fifths full. What is the capacity of the tank?

_____

37 One-fifth of the seats for a concert cost $45, one-third cost $30 and the remainder cost $20.

a What fraction of the seats cost $20?

_____

b If there are 210 seats at $20 how many people can be seated altogether?

_____

38 The local council agrees to pay $\frac{3}{7}$ of the cost of running a leisure centre, with central government paying the remainder. If the local council pays $420 000, find the total running cost.

_____

39 After spending $\frac{3}{7}$ of my money I have $204 remaining. How much did I have to start with?

_____

40 When the larger of two fractions is divided by the smaller one the answer is $1\frac{2}{5}$. If the larger fraction is $3\frac{1}{5}$, what is the smaller one?

_____

41 When 9 is divided by the product of two fractions the result is 1. If one of the fractions is $5\frac{2}{5}$, what is the other one?

_____

42 The product of two numbers is 8. If one of the numbers is $3\frac{1}{3}$, find the other one.

_____

43 The product of two numbers is 21. If one of the numbers is $2\frac{4}{7}$, find the other one.

_____

44 How many jars, each of which holds $\frac{3}{8}$ kg, may be filled from a tin containing 21 kg?

_____

45 If it takes $3\frac{1}{3}$ minutes to fill $\frac{3}{8}$ of a water storage tank, how long will it take to fill it completely?

_____

46 When the larger of two fractions is divided by the smaller, the result is $1\frac{7}{18}$. If the smaller fraction is $2\frac{2}{5}$, find the larger one.

_____

47 When the smaller of two fraction is divided by the larger, the result is $\frac{7}{9}$. If the smaller fraction is $2\frac{2}{3}$, find the larger one.

_____

1 What fraction of a revolution does the second hand of a clock turn through when:

   a it starts at 4 and stops at 7   _____

   b it starts at 5 and stops at 12   _____

   c it starts at 2 and stops at 11   _____

   d it starts at 9 and stops at 5   _____

   e it starts at 6 and stops at 12   _____

   f it starts at 7 and stops at 11? _____

2 Where does the second hand stop if:

   a it starts at 5 and turns through $\frac{1}{2}$ of a turn

   b it starts at 8 and turns through $\frac{3}{4}$ of a turn

   c it starts at 2 and turns through $\frac{2}{3}$ of a turn

   d it starts at 9 and turns through $\frac{5}{6}$ of a turn

   e it starts at 3 and turns through $\frac{1}{3}$ of a turn

   f it starts at 7 and turns through $\frac{5}{6}$ of a turn?

3 a If you stand facing east and turn anticlockwise through $\frac{1}{4}$ of a revolution, in which direction are you facing?

   b If you stand facing west and turn through half a revolution, in which direction are you facing?

   c If you stand facing north and turn through $1\frac{1}{2}$ revolutions, in which direction are you facing?

   d If you stand facing north and turn clockwise through $\frac{3}{4}$ of a revolution, in which direction are you facing?

   e If you stand facing west and turn anticlockwise through $\frac{1}{4}$ of a revolution, in which direction are you facing?

4 How many right angles does the second hand of a clock turn through when:

   a it starts at 1 and stops at 7   _____

   b it starts at 3 and stops at 3   _____

   c it starts at 10 and stops at 7   _____

   d it starts at 11 and stops at 8   _____

   e it starts at 2 and stops at 8? _____

5 How many right angles do you turn through if you:

   a face south and turn clockwise to face north

   b face west and turn anticlockwise to face north

   c face east and turn clockwise to face south?

6 What type of angle is each of the following?

a

b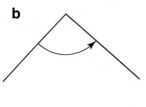

_____   _____

c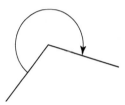

d

_____   _____

e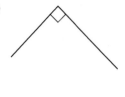

f

_____   _____

7 How many degrees has the second hand turned through when it moves from:

a 7 to 12   _____

b 6 to 2   _____

c 11 to 9? _____

8 Measure the following angles:

a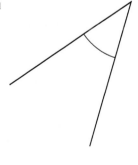

_____

b

_____

c

_____

d

_____

e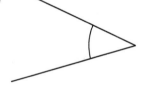

_____

f

_____

In questions **9** to **14**, find the size of the angle marked with a letter.

9 a 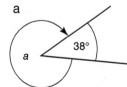 $a =$ _____

38°

b

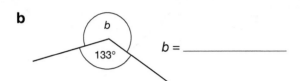

$b =$ _____

c

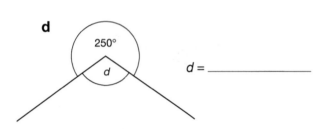

$c =$ _____

d

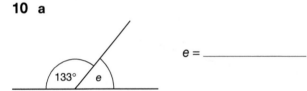

$d =$ _____

10 a

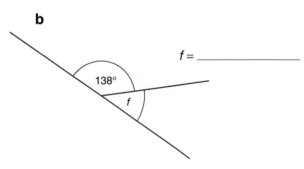

$e =$ _____

b

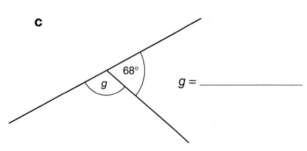

$f =$ _____

c

$g =$ _____

11

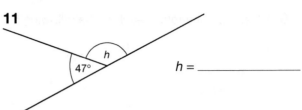

$h =$ _____

12

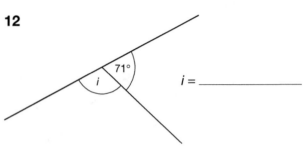

$i =$ _____

13

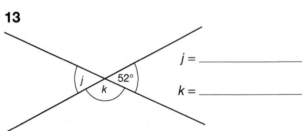

$j =$ _____

$k =$ _____

14 Find the size of each angle marked with a letter.

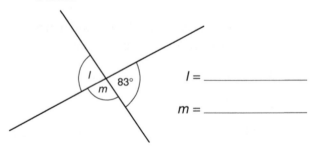

$l =$ _____

$m =$ _____

15 Which of these pairs of angles are complementary?

a 42° and 52° _____

b 35° and 55° _____

c 17° and 73° _____

d 72° and 28° _____

e 132° and 48° _____

f 96° and 86° _____

16 Which of these pairs of angles are supplementary?

a 150° and 30° _____

b 93° and 87° _____

c 46° and 144° _____

d 67° and 113° _____

e 140° and 50° _____

f 84° and 96° _____

17 Angles *a* and *b* are complementary.
Angle *a* is four times the size of *b*.
What is the size of *b*?

_____

18 Angles *c* and *d* are supplementary.
Angle *c* is five times the size of *d*.
What is the size of *c*?

_____

19 Angles *e* and *f* are complementary.
Angle *e* is 16° larger than *f*.
Find angle *f*.

_____

20 Angles *g* and *h* are supplementary.
Angle *g* is 48° smaller than *h*.
Find angles *g* and *h*.

_____

In questions **21** and **22**, write the pairs of angles that are supplementary.

21

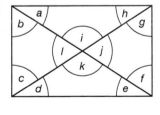

_____

_____

_____

22

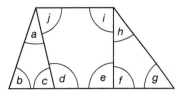

_____

_____

_____

_____

23 For each pair of angles say whether they are complementary angles, supplementary angles or neither:

a 132° and 48° _____

b 67° and 33° _____

c 74° and 106° _____

d 47° and 43° _____

e 93° and 97° _____

In questions **24** to **37**, find the size of each angle marked with a letter.

24

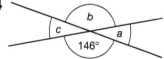

_____

_____

_____

25

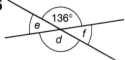

_____

_____

_____

26

_____

_____

_____

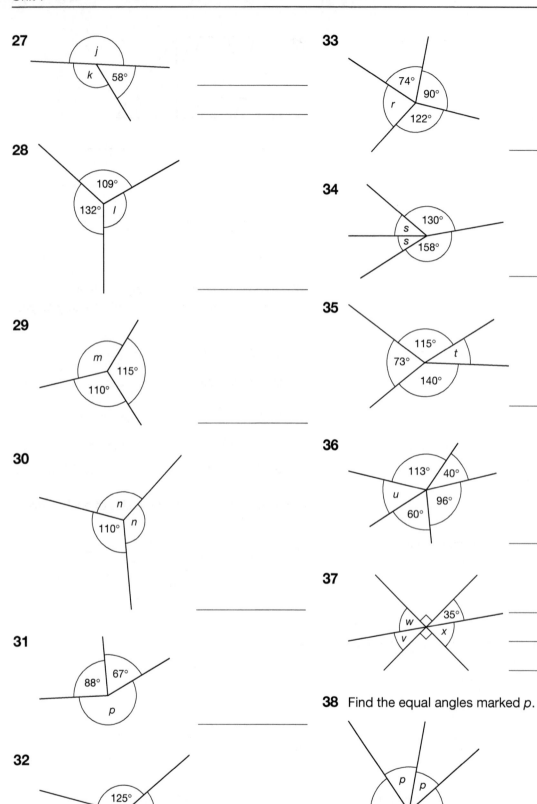

27

28

29

30

31

32

33

34

35

36

37

38 Find the equal angles marked *p*.

39 If angle *t* is twice angle *s*, find angle *u*.

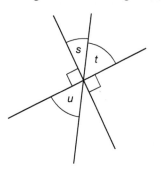

_____

40 The diagram shows three equal angles marked *x*. Find the size of angle *x* and go on to find the size of angle *y*.

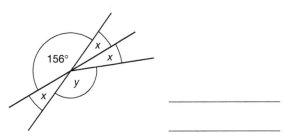

_____

_____

41 The diagram shows three intersecting straight lines. Find the size of the angles marked by letters.

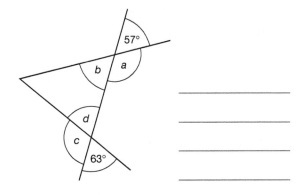

_____

_____

_____

_____

42 The angle marked *d* is 88°. Find the angle marked *e*.

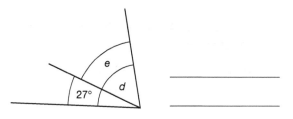

_____

_____

43 The angle at the vertex of the triangle is 90°. If angle *f* is twice angle *g*, find the angles *f*, *g* and *h*.

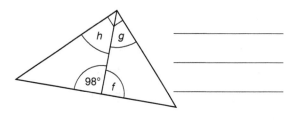

_____

_____

_____

In questions **1** to **14**, choose the letter that gives the correct answer.

1 To the nearest 100, 1549 is:

A 1500   **B** 1550

C 1600   **D** 1650

2 In the addition 53 + ☐9 = 102 the missing figure is:

A 1   **B** 3

C 4   **D** 5

3 The HCF of 8, 16 and 28 is:

A 4   **B** 8

C 56   **D** 112

4 The prime factors of 20 are:

A 2 and 4   **B** 2 and 10

C 2 and 5   **D** 4 and 5

5 The missing unit in the addition 2 m + 58☐ = 258 cm is:

A mm   **B** cm

C m   **D** km

6 The missing number in the subtraction 4.5 cm − ☐mm = 2.5 cm is:

A 0.2   **B** 2

C 20   **D** 200

7 $\dfrac{1}{2} \times \dfrac{5}{6} \div \dfrac{5}{21} =$

A $\dfrac{3}{7}$ **B** $\dfrac{7}{8}$

C $1\frac{2}{7}$ **D** $1\frac{3}{4}$

8 The LCM of 6, 9 and 24 is:

A 24   **B** 36

C 54   **D** 72

9 The value of $1^2 + 2^2 + 3^2$ is:

A 12   **B** 14

C 25   **D** 36

10 30 375 is exactly divisible by:

A 2 and 5   **B** 2 and 7

C 2 and 3   **D** 3 and 5

11 P = {whole numbers that divide exactly into 12}
Q = {whole numbers that divide exactly into 20}
P ∩ Q =

A {1, 2, 4}   **B** {2, 4}

C {2, 3}   **D** {2, 3, 4}

12 Look at the number 537 298 140. The digit that gives the number of tens of thousands is:

A 2   **B** 7

C 9   **D** 8

13 The value of the digit 5 in the number 6 573 982 is:

A 5 million   **B** 5 hundred thousand

C fifty thousand   **D** 5 thousand

14 Which one of the following statements is true?

A the next prime number after 43 is 49.

B there are only two prime numbers that are even numbers.

C there are six prime numbers between 4 and 20.

D the nearest prime number to 31 is 37

Use this diagram for questions **15** to **18**.

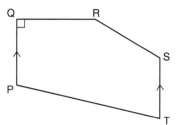

15 What name do we give to this shape?

_____

16 Name the two sides that are parallel.

_____

17 How many obtuse angles are there?

_____

18 Is any angle 90°? If so, name it.

_____

19 a Simplify $\dfrac{5}{12} \div \dfrac{15}{4}$

_____

  b Express 260 in prime factors.

_____

20 Given that $17\,290 = 2 \times 5 \times 7 \times 13 \times 19$:

  a does 19 divide exactly into 17 290? Why?

_____

  b does 49 divide exactly into 17 290? Why?

_____

  c does 38 divide exactly into 17 290? Why?

_____

21 Given that X = {factors of 54} and
  Y = {factors of 48}, list all the members of:

  a $X \cap Y$ _____

  b $X \cup Y$ _____

22 Using the figures 4, 5 and 6, write as
  many different three-figure numbers as you
  can. Put these numbers in order with the
  smallest first.

_____

23 Using the figures 7, 0 and 2 once in each
  number, write:

  a the largest number you can make

_____

  b the smallest number you can make

_____

c the difference between them.

_____

24 At the beginning of the day, a library had
  5637 books. During the day 623 books went
  out on loan and 774 were returned. How many
  books were there in the library at the end of
  the day?

_____

25 Find:

  a 1014×78 _____

  b $1014 \div 78$ _____

  c $1014 + 78$ _____

  d $1014 - 78$ _____

26 Find:

  a $15 \times 4 + 12 \div (9 - 5)$ _____

  b $15 + 4 - 12 \div (9 - 5)$ _____

  c $15 - 4 - 12 + (9 - 5)$ _____

  d $15 - 4 + 12 \times (9 + 5)$ _____

27 A book has 96 pages. Pages 47 to 62 are
  photographs. The remaining pages are all text,
  each of which has 38 lines with, on average,
  13 words in each line.

  a How many pages are just for photographs?

_____

  b How many pages are exclusively text?

_____

  c Roughly how many words are there on a
  page of text?

_____

  d Ken says that the book contains about
  40 000 words. Is he correct? Give a reason
  for your answer.

_____

28

a List the members in the set:

i A ∩ B _____

ii A ∪ B _____

b Describe the members in set A.

_____

c Describe the members in set B.

_____

29 In a class of 32 students, 12 take chemistry only, 8 take biology only, 10 take physics only while the remainder take none of these subjects. What fraction of the class:

a takes physics _____

b takes chemistry or biology _____

c does not take any of the named subjects?

_____

30 Write these numbers in order with the smallest first:

59 743, 128 850, 68 436, 9765, 73 429

_____

31 Use the digits 8, 5, 7, 3, 0, 9 once each, to make:

a the smallest possible number

_____

b the largest possible number.

_____

32 Find the value of:

3652
2987
1775
+7081

33 Find the value of:

65 583 + 356 000 + 30 068

_____

34 Add four hundred and fifty-seven, twenty-three hundred and six, and five thousand and thirteen.

_____

35 The combined population of Blackwood and Chesford is 54 738. If 21 745 live in Blackwood find:

a the population of Chesford

b how many more people live in Chesford than in Blackwood.

36 a Is 4031 divisible by 29?

_____

b State the LCM of 25, 30, 35.

_____

c State the HCF of 52, 65, 78.

_____

37 Write these statements in set notation:

a Albert Einstein belongs to the set of famous scientists.

_____

b Malaysia does not belong to the set of African countries.

_____

c Charlotte Bronte belongs to the set of famous novelists.

_____

d Mount Everest does not belong to the set of the world's oceans.

_____

38 If $P = \{p, q, r, s, t\}$ write all the subsets of P that have three members.

_____

39 Which of the following sets are empty sets?

    a {cattle with more than six legs}

    b {birds with four eyes}

    c {rivers more than 100 miles long}

    d {dogs with two tails}

40 Find the union of the two sets:

    A = {letters in the word FOREIGN}

    B = {letters in the word NATIVE}

41 Draw a suitable Venn diagram to show the union of the sets:

    P = {letters in the word PARLIAMENT}

    Q = {letters in the word DEMOCRACY}

42 Find the intersection of the following sets:

    A = {prime numbers smaller than 30}

    B = {odd numbers smaller than 30}

Use this cuboid to answer questions **43** to **46**.

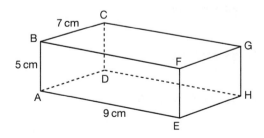

43 What meaning is given to the broken lines?

44 What are the measurements of the smallest face?

45 What is the total length of all its edges?

46 One of the longest straight lines that can be drawn on the surface of this solid is the straight line AH. How many other straight lines equal in length to AH can be drawn on the surface of this solid? Name them.

47 Fill in the missing numbers to make equivalent fractions:

    a $\dfrac{3}{7} = \dfrac{12}{\underline{}}$ **b** $\dfrac{5}{9} = \dfrac{\underline{}}{45}$

    c $\dfrac{2}{31} = \dfrac{8}{\underline{}}$ **d** $\dfrac{7}{8} = \dfrac{35}{\underline{}}$

48 Which fraction is the larger?

    a $\dfrac{5}{8}$ or $\dfrac{4}{7}$ _____   **b** $\dfrac{2}{3}$ or $\dfrac{7}{12}$ _____

    c $\dfrac{3}{4}$ or $\dfrac{9}{11}$ _____   **d** $\dfrac{8}{9}$ or $\dfrac{10}{11}$ _____

49 Arrange the following fractions in ascending order of size:

    $\dfrac{7}{10}, \dfrac{11}{25}, \dfrac{2}{5}, \dfrac{23}{50}, \dfrac{9}{10}$

50 Add these fractions, simplifying the answer if you can:

    $\dfrac{7}{12} + \dfrac{1}{12} + \dfrac{5}{12} + \dfrac{8}{12}$

51 Find:

a $\dfrac{1}{4}+\dfrac{5}{6}+\dfrac{7}{12}$ _____

b $\dfrac{1}{6}+\dfrac{2}{3}-\dfrac{4}{9}$ _____

52 Change these improper fractions to mixed numbers:

a $\dfrac{27}{4}$ _____   **b** $\dfrac{52}{7}$ _____   **c** $\dfrac{84}{11}$ _____

53 Change these mixed numbers to improper fractions:

a $7\frac{2}{3}$ _____   **b** $5\frac{2}{5}$ _____

c $13\frac{3}{7}$ _____

54 Calculate the following divisions, giving your answers as mixed numbers:

a $27 \div 4$ _____

b $23 \div 9$ _____

c $42 \div 13$ _____

55 Find:

a $6\frac{2}{3}+2\frac{5}{6}$ _____

b $3\frac{1}{2}+5\frac{9}{16}$ _____

c $3\frac{5}{14}+2\frac{4}{7}$ _____

56 Find:

a $8\frac{1}{4}-\frac{5}{8}$ _____

b $13\frac{7}{16}-8\frac{1}{2}$ _____

c $12\frac{5}{8}-4\frac{3}{4}$ _____

57 Find:

a $2\frac{3}{5}+6\frac{5}{6}-7\frac{7}{10}$ _____

b $5\frac{5}{12}-2\frac{3}{8}+1\frac{2}{3}$ _____

58 Find:

a $\dfrac{3}{4}\times\dfrac{7}{12}$ _____

b $\dfrac{5}{12}\times\dfrac{8}{9}$ _____

c $\dfrac{13}{20}\times\dfrac{8}{9}$ _____

59 Find:

a $6\frac{3}{5}\times\frac{5}{11}$ _____

b $5\frac{1}{3}\times\frac{9}{16}$ _____

c $\frac{3}{7}\times5\frac{5}{6}$ _____

60 Find:

a $\frac{3}{19}\times3\frac{1}{3}\times1\frac{9}{10}$ _____

b $1\frac{3}{5}\times3\frac{1}{4}\times1\frac{7}{13}$ _____

61 Find:

a $\frac{5}{8}$ of 480 cm _____

b $\frac{7}{11}$ of 165 days _____

c $\frac{4}{5}$ of 45 litres _____

d $\frac{5}{9}$ of \$540 _____

62 How many:

a $\frac{1}{3}$s are there in 3 _____

b $\frac{3}{4}$s are there in 15 _____

c $\frac{4}{5}$s are there in 20? _____

63 Find:

a $\frac{1}{4} \div 4$ _____

b $\frac{1}{8} \div \frac{1}{4}$ _____

c $2 \div \frac{2}{9}$ _____

d $\frac{3}{4} \div 3$ _____

64 Find:

a $2\frac{1}{2} \div \frac{2}{5}$ _____

b $4\frac{1}{2} \div 1\frac{7}{20}$ _____

c $3\frac{2}{5} \div 4\frac{1}{4}$ _____

65 When 5 is divided by the product of two fractions the result is 2. One of the fractions is $4\frac{1}{3}$. What is the other?

_____

66 After spending $\frac{5}{9}$ of my money I have $180 left. How much did I have to start with?

_____

67 The product of two numbers is 12. If one number is $1\frac{7}{9}$ what is the other?

_____

68 It took me 3 minutes to read 40 lines of a book. At the same rate how long should it take me to read:

a 100 lines _____

b 500 lines? _____

69 What fraction of a revolution does the 'seconds' hand of a clock turn through if:

a it starts at 3 and stops at 12 _____

b it starts at 10 and stops at 4 _____

c it starts at 12 and stops at 11? _____

70 What type of angle is each of the following?

a

_____

b

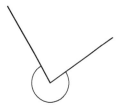

_____

c

_____

71 a If you stand facing south and turn clockwise through half a revolution, in which direction are you facing?

_____

b If you stand facing east and turn anticlockwise through three-quarters of a revolution, in which direction are you facing?

_____

c If you stand facing north and turn clockwise through 90°, in which direction are you facing?

_____

In questions **72** to **77**, find the size of each of the angles marked with letters.

72

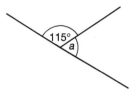

76

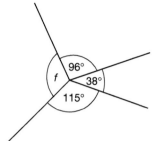

73

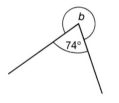

77

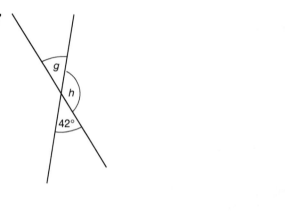

74

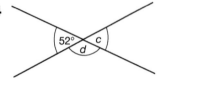

75

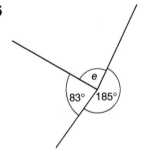

8 Introduction to decimals

1 What is the value of the figure 4 in each of the following numbers?

  a 34.7 _____

  b 65.4 _____

  c 48.2 _____

  d 85.04 _____

2 What is value of the figure 7 in each of the following numbers?

  a 70.6 _____

  b 4.76 _____

  c 13.07 _____

  d 67.09 _____

3 Write each set of numbers in order of size with the smallest first:

  a 7.6, 7.06, 7.77 _____

  b 31.72, 37.21, 32.17, 31.27 _____

  c 9.42, 9.14, 9.24, 9.22 _____

4 Write each set of numbers in order of size with the smallest first:

  a 3.6, 3.06, 3.66 _____

  b 54.65, 55.09, 55.90, 54.88 _____

  c 8.54, 8.09, 8.86, 8.45 _____

  d 26.3, 2.77, 25.9, 2.99 _____

5 Write as fractions:

  a 0.83 _____

  b 0.41 _____

  c 0.013 _____

  d 0.0071 _____

  e 0.0211 _____

6 Write as fractions:

  a 0.43 _____

  b 0.11 _____

  c 0.019 _____

  d 0.0029 _____

  e 0.0028 _____

7 Write as fractions in their lowest terms:

  a 0.75 _____

  b 0.8 _____

  c 0.64 _____

  d 0.0035 _____

  e 0.16 _____

8 Write as fractions in their lowest terms:

  a 0.65 _____

  b 0.36 _____

  c 0.94 _____

  d 0.072 _____

  e 0.0028 _____

9 **a** How many tenths must be added to 7.3 to make a total of 8? _____

  b How many hundredths must be added to 4.48 to make a total of 5? _____

  c How many tenths must be added to 16.8 to make 19? _____

10 **a** How many tenths must be added to 12.7 to make a total of 13? _____

  b How many hundredths must be added to 8.46 to make a total of 9? _____

c How many tenths must be subtracted from 16.2 to make 15? _____

d How many hundreds must be subtracted from 4.66 to make 4? _____

11 Write the following fractions as decimals:

  a $\dfrac{9}{100}$ _____

  b $\dfrac{17}{100}$ _____

  c $3\frac{7}{10}$ _____

  d $9\frac{31}{1000}$ _____

  e $8\frac{7}{10}$ _____

12 Write the following fractions as decimals:

  a $\dfrac{3}{100}$ _____

  b $\dfrac{19}{100}$ _____

  c $5\frac{17}{100}$ _____

  d $7\frac{37}{1000}$ _____

13 Find:

  a $4.72 + 1.26$ _____

  b $0.15 + 0.15$ _____

  c $8.2 + 0.004$ _____

  d $3.45 + 0.742$ _____

  e $0.64 + 0.064 + 0.006$ _____

14 Find:

  a $7.38 + 2.54$ _____

  b $0.39 + 0.39$ _____

  c $5.6 + 0.004$ _____

  d $2.66 + 0.634$ _____

  e $0.46 + 0.046 + 0.0046$ _____

15 Find:

  a $10 - 7.2$ _____

  b $8.6 - 5.4$ _____

  c $6.92 - 1.09$ _____

  d $105.7 - 58.6$ _____

  e $7.5 - 2.92$ _____

  f $0.03 - 0.00071$ _____

  g $9 - 0.00736$ _____

16 Find:

  a $12 - 5.73$ _____

  b $4.7 - 1.5$ _____

  c $8.44 - 3.78$ _____

  d $209.5 - 178.6$ _____

  e $5.3 - 3.84$ _____

17 Find:

  a $5.4 - 2.6 + 8.5$ _____

  b $1.3 + 13 - 0.13$ _____

  c $86 - 3.45 - 17.2$ _____

  d $5.6 + 0.33 - 4.008$ _____

  e $3.7 - 0.043 + 5.9$ _____

  f $80 - 45.21 - 19.66$ _____

  g $12.05 + 3.007 - 1.88$ _____

18 Find:

  a $3.7 + 6.3 - 6.2$ _____

  b $2.6 + 2.06 - 2.36$ _____

  c $54 - 31.7 - 4.33$ _____

  d $8.3 + 0.66 - 5.39$ _____

19 One book costs $44.99 and another book costs $37.95.

   a How much do the two books cost together?

_____

   b How much change will I get if I pay with a $100 note?

_____

20 One drink costs $6.75 and another drink cost $7.99.

   a How much do the two drinks cost together?

_____

   b How much change will I get if I pay with a $20 note?

_____

21 a Find the total cost of three articles costing $4.50, $13.75 and $16.84. _____

   b I pay with two $20 bills. How much change do I get? _____

22 Add 15.4 to 7.03 and subtract the total from 30.

_____

23 Add 13.7 to 9.8 and subtract the total from 42.

_____

24 What is the perimeter of this quadrilateral?

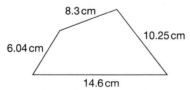

25 The perimeter of this triangle is 30 cm. Work out the length of the third side.

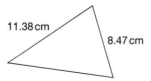

_____

26 The length of the perimeter of this quadrilateral is 30.5 cm. What is the length of the unmarked side?

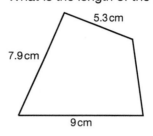

_____

27 Find the value of:

   a 26.44×100 _____

   b 0.033×10 _____

   c $2 \div 100$ _____

   d $0.7 \div 1000$ _____

   e 0.055×100 _____

   f $14 \div 10000$ _____

28 Find the value of:

   a 45.3×10 _____

   b 0.004×1000 _____

   c $12 \div 100$ _____

   d $0.3 \div 10$ _____

   e $346 \div 1000$ _____

29 Find the cost of 100 articles at $2.47 each.

_____

30 Find the cost of 50 articles at $5.99 each.

_____

31 Wall tiles are 0.45 cm thick. How high is a pile of 24 tiles?

_____

32 Find the value of:

   a $614.3 \div 100$ _____

   b $87 \div 10$ _____

c $4.21 \div 1000$ _____

d $0.0005 \div 100$ _____

33 Find the value of:

    a $546.8 \div 1000$ _____

    b $34 \div 100$ _____

    c $7.61 \div 1000$ _____

    d $0.08 \div 10$ _____

    e $0.003 \div 100$ _____

34 Divide 5.7 by 1000 and multiply the result by 10.

_____

35 Divide 64 by 10000 and multiply the result by 10.

_____

36 Divide 0.016 by 4 and multiply the result by 100.

_____

37 Subtract 0.7 from 3 and multiply the result by 100.

_____

38 Take 0.26 from 1.55 and divide the result by 100.

_____

39 Find the value of:

    a $1.8 \div 6$ _____

    b $27.5 \div 5$ _____

    c $0.0028 \div 4$ _____

    d $292 \div 8$ _____

    e $0.0618 \div 6$ _____

40 Find the value of:

    a $2.4 \div 8$ _____

    b $58.5 \div 5$ _____

c $0.0072 \div 6$ _____

d $10.29 \div 7$ _____

e $19.60 \div 8$ _____

41 Find the value of:

    a $40.5 \div 15$ _____

    b $77.4 \div 43$ _____

    c $81.6 \div 17$ _____

    d $7.28 \div 14$ _____

    e $15.4 \div 28$ _____

42 Find the value of:

    a $40.8 \div 12$ _____

    b $94.5 \div 35$ _____

    c $154.5 \div 103$ _____

    d $1.38 \div 23$ _____

    e $18.86 \div 41$ _____

43 The perimeter of a square is 9.64 cm. What is the length of one side?

_____

44 The perimeter of a regular pentagon is 18.5 cm. Work out the length of one side.

_____

45 Divide $39.76 equally between seven students.

_____

46 Express the following fractions as decimals:

    a $\dfrac{3}{4}$ _____

    b $\dfrac{9}{16}$ _____

    c $7\frac{3}{5}$ _____

    d $\dfrac{3}{32}$ _____

e $\dfrac{35}{4}$ _____

f $\dfrac{16}{5}$ _____

47 Express the following fractions as decimals:

a $\dfrac{7}{8}$ _____

b $\dfrac{5}{16}$ _____

c $5\dfrac{3}{10}$ _____

d $\dfrac{47}{4}$ _____

e $\dfrac{22}{5}$ _____

48 Divide 63 by 15.

_____

49 Divide 0.34 by ten thousand.

_____

50 Express $\dfrac{9}{16}$ as a decimal.

_____

51 Divide 3.5 by 25.

_____

52 Express 5.016 as a mixed number in its lowest terms.

_____

53 Divide 0.66 by a thousand.

_____

54 Express 8.064 as a mixed number in its lowest terms.

_____

55 My electricity bill for air conditioning and lighting was $324. If $\dfrac{7}{9}$ of the cost was for air conditioning, how much did I pay for lighting?

_____

56 The sum of two adjacent sides of a square is 14.7 cm.

a What is the length of one side?

_____

b What is the perimeter of this square?

_____

57 Marsha has $24.50 in her purse. She buys two articles costing $8.95 each and one article costing $5.75. How much money does she have left after this transaction?

_____

58 The perimeter of a regular polygon with eight sides is 27.6 cm. What is the length of one side?

_____

59 From a plank of wood 5 metres long, Lloyd cuts one piece 1.8 metres long and another piece 2.46 metres long. What length remains?

_____

60 From a jug holding $1\dfrac{1}{2}$ litres of water Millie fills two glasses, each holding 0.275 litres. How much water remains in the jug?

_____

61 How many glasses each holding 0.24 litres can be filled from a bottle holding 2 litres?

_____

9 Multiplication and division of decimals

1 Calculate the following products:

  a 0.04×0.5 _____

  b 4×0.4 _____

  c 0.7×0.006 _____

  d 0.006×0.003 _____

2 Calculate the following products:

  a 0.06×0.4 _____

  b 5×0.6 _____

  c 0.4×0.003 _____

  d 0.007×0.002 _____

3 Calculate the following products:

  a 5.6×0.2 _____

  b 39×0.32 _____

  c 0.13×14 _____

  d 1.8×8.1 _____

  e 7.3×5.6 _____

4 Calculate the following products:

  a 3.8×0.3 _____

  b 54×0.42 _____

  c 0.19×0.18 _____

  d 8.2×2.6 _____

5 Find the cost of 10 toys at $23.55 each.

_____

6 Find the cost of 4 meals at $12.99 each.

_____

7 Multiply 2.8 by 6 and divide the result by 7.

_____

8 Divide 25.8 by 6 and multiply the result by 5.

_____

9 The length of a side of a regular pentagon is 3.45 cm. Work out the perimeter of the pentagon.

_____

10 Divide 27.3 kg into seven equal parts.

_____

11 Divide 38.4 into eight equal parts.

_____

12 Find the cost of 4.5 metres of material at $14.60 per metre.

_____

13 A fence, 48 metres long, is to be erected along one side of a vegetable garden. Clive erects 17 posts which are equally spaced. What is the distance between consecutive posts?

_____

14 Use dot notation to write these fractions as decimals:

  a $\dfrac{8}{9}$ _____

  b $\dfrac{5}{11}$ _____

  c $\dfrac{4}{7}$ _____

  d $\dfrac{13}{7}$ _____

15 Use dot notation to write these fractions as decimals:

  a $\dfrac{2}{11}$ _____

  b $\dfrac{5}{7}$ _____

c $\frac{4}{13}$ _____

d $\frac{9}{7}$ _____

16 Give 23.6754 correct to:

a the nearest whole number _____

b one decimal place _____

c three decimal places. _____

17 Give 543.847 correct to:

a the nearest whole number _____

b two decimal places _____

c one decimal place. _____

18 Give the following numbers correct to the nearest whole number:

a 17.4 _____

b 6.987 _____

c 64.099 _____

19 Give the following numbers correct to the nearest whole number:

a 9.909 _____

b 3.376 _____

c 17.505 _____

20 Give the following numbers correct to three decimal places:

a 47.4756 _____

b 6.9875 _____

c 64.090909 _____

21 Give the following numbers correct to two decimal places:

a 15.4747 _____

b 0.0389 _____

c 6.0505 _____

22 Give the following numbers correct to the number of decimal places indicated in the brackets:

a 0.099 (1) _____

b 0.0075 (2) _____

c 2.161 616 (3) _____

d 0.198 165 (3) _____

e 7.9858 (3) _____

23 Give the following numbers correct to the number of decimal places indicated in brackets:

a 0.0777 (2) _____

b 6.167 167 (3) _____

c 0.837 45 (3) _____

d 12.2826 (1) _____

e 3.0352 (2) _____

24 Express 67.459 correct to:

a the nearest whole number _____

b one decimal place _____

c two decimal places. _____

25 Express 49.837 correct to:

a the nearest whole number _____

b one decimal place _____

c two decimal places. _____

26 Calculate the following, giving your answers correct to two decimal places:

a $0.547 \div 3$ _____

b $23.86 \div 9$ _____

c $37.4 \div 26$ _____

27 Calculate the following, giving your answers correct to two decimal places:

a $1.67 \div 7$ _____

b $16.46 \div 9$ _____

c $24.85 \div 21$ _____

28 Calculate the following, giving your answers correct to one decimal place:

a $302 \div 7$ _____

b $223 \div 15$ _____

c $419 \div 19$ _____

29 Calculate the following, giving your answers correct to three decimal places:

a $0.041 \div 7$ _____

b $0.85 \div 32$ _____

c $1.29 \div 13$ _____

30 Give these fractions as exact decimals:

a $\dfrac{3}{8}$ _____

b $\dfrac{11}{16}$ _____

c $\dfrac{7}{80}$ _____

31 Give these fractions as exact decimals:

a $\dfrac{9}{16}$ _____

b $\dfrac{17}{40}$ _____

c $\dfrac{9}{20}$ _____

32 Give these fractions as decimals correct to three decimal places:

a $\dfrac{3}{7}$ _____

b $\dfrac{5}{11}$ _____

c $\dfrac{1}{13}$ _____

33 Give these fractions as decimals correct to three decimal places:

a $\dfrac{5}{6}$ _____

b $\dfrac{2}{9}$ _____

c $\dfrac{8}{21}$ _____

34 Find the exact answer for these questions:

a $0.12 \div 0.2$ _____

b $0.7 \div 0.007$ _____

c $1.92 \div 2.4$ _____

d $0.000513 \div 0.03$ _____

e $9.1 \div 1.4$ _____

35 Find the exact answer for these questions:

a $0.18 \div 4$ _____

b $0.8 \div 0.25$ _____

c $0.000478 \div 8$ _____

d $8.64 \div 2.4$ _____

36 Find the exact answer for these questions:

a 0.84×0.4 _____

b 3.47×0.7 _____

c 13.4×0.6 _____

d 9.2×0.03 _____

37 Find the exact answer for these questions:

a 8.26×0.5 _____

b 5.67×0.3 _____

c 15.8×0.8 _____

d 6.3×0.04 _____

e 0.07×3.92 _____

38 Find the value of:

a $\dfrac{0.3 \times 0.6}{0.8}$ _____

b $\dfrac{5.5 \times 3}{11}$ _____

c $\dfrac{5.5 \times 0.3}{11}$ _____

39 Find the value of:

a $\dfrac{0.4 \times 0.8}{0.5}$ _____

b $\dfrac{4.2 \times 4}{7}$ _____

c $\dfrac{4.2 \times 0.4}{0.07}$ _____

40 Calculate, giving your answer correct to the number of decimal places shown in brackets:

a $0.456 \div 7$ (2) _____

b $15 \div 11$ (3) _____

c $1.36 \div 1.3$ (2) _____

d $0.35 \div 1.2$ (1) _____

e $0.0067 \div 0.031$ (4) _____

41 Calculate, giving your answer correct to the number of decimal places shown in brackets:

a $1.69 \div 8$ (2) _____

b $18 \div 13$ (3) _____

c $3.36 \div 2.3$ (2) _____

d $0.94 \div 3.1$ (1) _____

42 Multiply 2.64 by 0.492. Give your answer correct to three decimal places.

_____

43 Multiply 5.63 by 0.652. Give your answer correct to three decimal places.

_____

44 Pauline's car travels 94.5 km on 7.5 litres of petrol. How many kilometres per litre is this?

_____

45 Curtain material costs $26.55 a metre. How many complete metres of curtain material may be bought for $350? What sum of money is left over?

_____

46 Tyres for my car cost $680.50 each. How much will a set of four tyres cost me? I go to the garage with six $500 notes. Will this be enough, and if so, by how much?

_____

47 Find:

a 4.8×0.4 _____

b $4.8 \div 0.04$ _____

c $0.48 \div 40$ _____

d 0.048×40 _____

48 A truck has a mass of 2.54 tonnes. It is loaded with 30 boxes, each box having a mass of 0.046 tonnes. Find:

a the total mass of the boxes _____

b the total mass of the loaded truck. _____

49 a How many packs, each containing 450 g, can be filled from a crate containing three-quarters of a tonne of mixed fruit?

_____

b How much remains? _____

50 The instructions on a bag of fertiliser state that it should be used at the rate of 0.04 kg to the square metre. How many square metres will a 2 kg bag of fertiliser cover?

51 A dining table costs $3450.50, a dining chair $755.50 and a dining chair with arms (a carver) $990.50. What would be the total cost of a table and eight chairs, two of which are carvers?

52 A bottle holds 0.7 litres of squash. How many glasses can be filled from this bottle, if each glass holds 0.0875 litres?

53 From a 500 cm length of tape, Grace cuts pieces 31.25 cm long. How many complete pieces does she get?

54 On average, each cow in a herd of 55 gives 18.8 litres of milk a day. How much milk should this herd produce:

a in a day

b in a week?

Give each answer correct to the nearest 10 litres.

55 Last week Norma earned $769.50 after working for 37.5 hours. How much was this per hour?

56 Tablets, each of mass 0.54 grams, are packed into foil strips, each strip containing 24 tablets. A box contains four foil strips and 250 boxes are packed into a carton. What is the mass of the tablets in the carton?

57 Work out the cost of 9.38 metres of material at $7.55 per metre. (Give your answer correct to the nearest cent.)

58 Table salt is sold in boxes of mass 1.5 kg. If a salt cellar requires 35.5 g of salt to fill it, how many times can it be filled from one box of table salt? Give your answer correct to the nearest whole number.

59 If 2.54 cm equals 1 inch, and 12 inches equals one foot, express 10 000 cm in feet, correct to the nearest foot.

60 If I give 0.375 of my ball of string to my sister, then half of what remains to my brother, I still have 4.3 m remaining. What length of string did I have to start with?

61 How many ball-bearings, each of mass 6.25 g, have a total mass of 800 g?

62 Shazad can buy packets of chocolate-coated brazil nuts at a cost of $2.33 for each packet.

a How many packets can he buy for $40?

b How much change will Shazad get?

1 The shoe sizes of a group of boys were recorded as:

6　10　$6\frac{1}{2}$　9　$6\frac{1}{2}$　6　8　$6\frac{1}{2}$　10　10　$7\frac{1}{2}$　$7\frac{1}{2}$

$6\frac{1}{2}$　7　7　$10\frac{1}{2}$　$7\frac{1}{2}$　7　$8\frac{1}{2}$　$8\frac{1}{2}$　9　$7\frac{1}{2}$　$9\frac{1}{2}$　$7\frac{1}{2}$

7　11　7　7　$8\frac{1}{2}$　9　$8\frac{1}{2}$　$6\frac{1}{2}$　6　8　8　$8\frac{1}{2}$

9　8　8　$9\frac{1}{2}$　9　$9\frac{1}{2}$　$9\frac{1}{2}$　10　8　$10\frac{1}{2}$　$7\frac{1}{2}$　8

Complete this frequency table.

Shoe size	Tally	Frequency
6		
$6\frac{1}{2}$		
7		
$7\frac{1}{2}$		
8		
$8\frac{1}{2}$		
9		
$9\frac{1}{2}$		
10		
$10\frac{1}{2}$		
11		

2 A group of boys played football every day after school.
The table shows the number of goals scored each day.

Weekday	Mon	Tues	Wed	Thurs	Fri
Number of goals scored	8	4	6	3	5

Draw a bar chart to show this information.

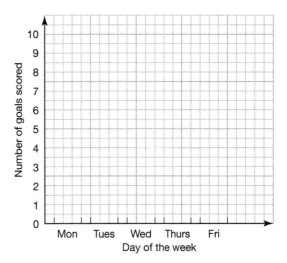

3 The marks of 60 students in an English examination are given below.

70　42　77　58　55　60　49　57　30　76
59　87　64　24　65　35　64　48　93　57
56　66　76　43　82　44　73　80　62　42
71　79　56　34　57　76　18　32　58　39
84　65　63　75　95　43　71　85　27　69
31　14　43　63　70　61　84　66　62　75

Use this data to complete the following grouped frequency table.

Mark	Tally	Frequency
11–20		
21–30		
31–40		
41–50		
51–60		
61–70		
71–80		
81–90		
91–100		

4 The following numbers give the mass in kilograms (to the nearest kg) of 80 mangoes gathered from one tree:

142 195 224 194 150 192 228 133 186 165

201 194 159 187 210 186 163 233 162 111

209 187 115 187 146 120 236 197 184 252

133 197 195 181 207 165 175 151 183 217

185 182 132 174 127 174 209 187 219 155

179 195 229 165 143 205 165 119 192 215

143 184 174 192 255 117 237 159 172 149

219 246 156 166 203 193 165 128 189 212

For this data complete this frequency table.

Mass to nearest kilogram	Tally	Frequency
100–119		
120–139		
140–159		
160–179		
180–199		
200–219		
220–239		
240–259		

5 On graph paper, draw a bar chart to show the information given in the frequency table which shows the number of children in each of the families in a street.

Number of children	0	1	2	3	4	5	6
Frequency	8	4	9	6	3	0	1

6 The times in minutes taken by a group of students to complete a test are given in the table.

Time (minutes)	45	46	47	48	49	50	51
Number of pupils	2	4	5	8	7	3	1

a How many students are there in the group?

_____

b On graph paper, draw a bar chart to represent this information. _____

c Which time occurs most often? _____

d What fraction of the group complete the test in less than 47 minutes? _____

e What percentage of the group complete the test in less than 47 minutes? _____

7 Indrani is given a packet of stamps as a birthday present. The stamps come from Aruba, Barbados, China, Dominica, Egypt, France and Grenada, represented by the letters A to G.

F D A A A A F F F F F B

B C G F A A F A A C D G

E A A A G D G C A G F C

B C G G F A A F A A C D

E A A A G D G C A G F C

a Compose a tally table for this data.

b Put these results into this frequency table.

Country	A	B	C	D	E	F	G
Frequency							

8 This bar chart shows, by percentage, the amount of people from different countries that visit the USA as tourists.

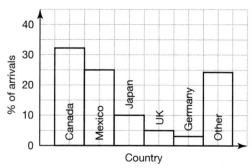

a Which country provided the most tourists?

_____

b Estimate the percentage of the tourists that came from Mexico.

_____

c Did Japan provide more tourists than the UK and Germany put together?

_____

9 This pictogram shows the choice of main course at Lisette's Café one lunch time.

Jerk chicken	🍽 🍽 🍽 🍽
Saltfish	🍽 🍽 🍽 🍽 🍽 🍽 🍽 🍽
Goat stew	🍽 🍽 🍽 🍽 🍽 🍽
Papaya salad	🍽 🍽 🍽

Key: 🍽 = 5 servings

a i What was the most popular choice?

_____

ii How many of this course were chosen?

_____

b i What was the least popular choice?

_____

ii How many of this course were chosen?

_____

c How many main courses were served in total?

_____

d How many more saltfish than jerk chicken main courses were served?

_____

10 The pictogram shows the number of books sold in a charity shop during the first four weeks after it opened.

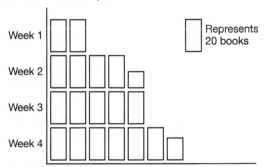

a How many books were sold the first week?

_____

b How many books were sold during the fourth week?

_____

c How many more books were sold during the third week than during the second week?

_____

d How many books were sold altogether?

_____

11 Find the arithmetic average (or mean) of the following sets of numbers:

a 3, 6, 8, 10, 18 _____

b 14, 16, 19, 23, 28 _____

c 35, 47, 12, 16, 55 _____

d 3.2, 4.5, 2.8, 5.2, 1.9, 2.8 _____

e 0.44, 0.73, 0.63, 0.62, 0.56, 0.53, 0.13

_____

12 A cricketer took 94 wickets for 1457 runs. Work out his average number of runs per wicket.

_____

13 The recorded rainfall each day while I was on holiday was: 2.5 mm, 0, 0, 4 mm, 5.5 mm, 0, 4.1 mm. Find the mean daily rainfall for the week.

_____

14 A batsman scored 924 runs in 28 completed innings. Find the average number of runs per innings.

_____

15 The masses, in kilograms, of the 11 men in a cricket team are 65.4, 73.6, 72.1, 68.4, 77.3, 68.7, 64.2, 71.9, 72.1, 69.5, 75.6. Find the average mass of the members in the team.

_____

16 On average my car travels 12.5 km on each litre of fuel. How far should I be able to go on 82 litres?

_____

17 The average number of hours of sunshine each day during my 14-day holiday was 7.4. How many hours of sunshine were there altogether?

_____

18 I spent the month of September in Kingston, Jamaica. The average daily rainfall was 3.3 mm. How much rain fell during the month?

_____

19 Sally took part in a sponsored run. The first 11 people agreed to sponsor her, on average, for $3.50. After the 12th person sponsored her, the average amount had increased to $3.80. For how much did the 12th person agree to sponsor her?

_____

20 The average height of 14 players in a football squad is 177 cm. As a result of a fifteenth boy joining, the average height of the squad drops to 176 cm. What is the height of the player who joins?

_____

21 Tickets for a concert, which is a sell-out, are priced at $35 and $50. Sales figures show that 60 of the more expensive tickets were sold and 250 tickets were sold altogether.

a What was the total income? _____

b What was the mean ticket price?

_____

22 After 9 tests Gino's average percentage mark was 63. This increased to 65 when he got his mark for maths. Find his mark for maths.

_____

23 Find the mode of each of the following sets of numbers:

a 0, 1, 4, 3, 3, 4, 2, 1, 5, 4, 5, 5, 0, 4, 4, 5, 2

_____

b 13, 12, 12, 15, 14, 15, 12, 13, 13, 15, 14, 15, 12, 13, 14, 15 _____

c 72, 69, 68, 72, 65, 69, 74, 73, 72, 73, 68, 73, 69, 74, 69 _____

d $4\frac{1}{2}$, 4, 5, 6, $5\frac{1}{2}$, $4\frac{1}{2}$, 6, 7, $7\frac{1}{2}$, 8, 4, 6, 5, 8, $5\frac{1}{2}$, $4\frac{1}{2}$ _____

e 7.8, 8.1, 7.7, 8.4, 8.1, 8.4, 7.7, 7.9, 7.5, 7.9, 8.1 _____

24 The number of photographs on the first 25 pages of a book are:
2, 4, 4, 0, 0, 2, 3, 5, 0, 0, 2, 4, 0, 2, 2, 0, 5, 7, 0, 0, 2, 2, 0, 0, 2

a How many photographs are there on the first 25 pages of the book?

_____

b What is the modal number of photographs per page?

_____

25 The colours used to paint the houses in my street are: white, blue, pink, white, blue, red, blue, pink, yellow, green, pink, white, blue, red, pink, red, blue, green.

a How many houses are there in my street?

_____

b What is the modal colour? _____

26 Given below are the marks out of 10 scored by the pupils in a geography test:
6, 8, 6, 6, 5, 8, 7, 4, 9, 10, 9, 8, 6, 8, 9, 6, 7, 8, 6, 7, 8, 8, 5, 7, 8, 10, 9, 8, 7, 6

a On graph paper, draw a bar chart to show this information.

b What is the modal mark? _____

27 The guests at a hotel were asked how many rooms there were in their home. Their answers are shown in the table.

Number of rooms	3	4	5	6	7	8
Frequency	8	18	19	27	4	3

  a How many guests were there at the hotel?

  _____

  b Find the mean number of rooms in the

  homes of the guests. _____

  _____

In questions **28** to **32**, find the mean, the mode and the median for each of the following sets of numbers:

28 32, 19, 14, 25, 17, 19

  Mean _____ Mode _____

  Median _____

29 70, 83, 71, 67, 81, 67, 69, 68, 72

  Mean _____ Mode _____

  Median _____

30 12, 13, 16, 14, 15, 16, 14, 13, 17, 16, 17, 17, 12, 16, 16, 17, 14

  Mean _____ Mode _____

  Median _____

31 35, 53, 22, 3, 18, 6, 3, 83, 74

  Mean _____ Mode _____

  Median _____

32 110, 107, 112, 107, 108, 107, 106, 107

  Mean _____ Mode _____

  Median _____

33 Find the median of each of the following sets of numbers:

  a 7, 9, 13, 17, 21

  _____

  b 5, 47, 36, 28, 51, 34, 44

  _____

  c 12, 19, 37, 72, 14, 42

  _____

  d 1.88, 1.92, 1.87, 1.78, 1.94, 1.86

  _____

  e 63.5, 64.2, 67.5, 57.6, 63.7, 64.6, 63.8

  _____

  f 6, 4, 5, 4, 4, 8, 3, 10, 7, 5, 2, 9, 8, 5, 9, 6, 8, 7, 3, 6, 5, 6, 7, 8, 8, 9, 9

  _____

34 The percentage marks in a maths exam for the pupils in a class are:
76, 89, 67, 56, 77, 83, 85, 73, 73, 46, 78, 92, 86, 83, 82, 75, 74, 78, 85, 65.

Rewrite these marks in ascending order and hence find the median mark.

_____

35 The heights (correct to the nearest centimetre) of a group of young people are:
154, 155, 158, 163, 153, 161, 160, 156, 162, 158. Find:

  a their mean height _____

  b their modal height _____

  c their median height. _____

36 Find the mean, mode and median of each set of numbers:

  a 10, 8, 12, 15, 14, 13, 12

    Mean _____ Mode _____

    Median _____

  b 1.4, 1.8, 1.7, 1.2, 1.2, 1.3, 1.2

    Mean _____ Mode _____

    Median _____

  c 2.8, 1.7, 2.7, 2.5, 3.1, 2.9, 3.4, 2.1

    Mean _____ Mode _____

    Median _____

37 A school entered 8 girls in a swimming competition. The marks they scored were: 72, 95, 85, 43, 75, 82, 63, 59. Find:

a the mean mark _____

b the median mark _____

c Does the mean or median give the best representation of the group as a whole? (Briefly explain why.)

_____

_____

38 Stuart was reading a book. He counted the number of letters in the words of a paragraph. They were:

2 5 7 5 2 8 8 7 6 3
4 7 6 12 1 7 13 9 9 8
5 9 4 6 6 9 3 10 12 7

a How many words were there in the paragraph? _____

For the data find:

b the mean number of letters per word

_____

c the mode _____

d the median. _____

39 A gymnastics competition was marked out of 40. This stem-and-leaf diagram shows the marks scored by all the competitors.

(1 | 2 means 12)

1 | 2 4 4 5 6 6 8 8 8

2 | 3 3 3 5 5 7 9

3 | 1 4 5 6

a How many competitors were there?

_____

b Write:

i the highest mark _____

ii the lowest mark. _____

c Find the median mark. _____

d Calculate the mean mark. _____

40 The table shows the number of tickets bought per person for a pop concert by the first group of people in a queue.

No. of tickets bought	1	2	3	4	5	6	8
Frequency	300	250	120	45	3	10	2

a How many people were in the first group to buy tickets? _____

b Find the mean number of tickets bought.

_____

c Find the mode. _____

41 This table shows the number of plants bought by the customers at a garden centre.

Number of plants	1	2	3	4	5	6
Frequency	15	21	8	5	3	1

Find:

a the mean number of plants bought

_____

b the modal number. _____

42 Four coins were flipped together 40 times and the number of heads per throw was recorded in the following table.

No. of heads	0	1	2	3	4
Frequency	3	10	17	8	2

Find:

a the median number of heads per throw

_____

b the mode _____

c the mean. _____

43 Dr Ali recorded the number of patients he saw each hour over a period of a week. The data are given in the following table.

Number of patients	4	5	6	7	8	9	10
Frequency	5	8	12	8	7	3	4

a How many patients did he see?

b For the data find:

   i the median _____

   ii the mode _____

   iii the mean. _____

44 The number of letters delivered one morning to each of the houses in a street are given in the table below.

House number	1	2	3	4	5	6	7	8	9	10
Number of letters	0	1	0	7	3	1	0	4	1	0

House number	11	12	13	14	15	16	17	18	19	20
Number of letters	1	0	1	3	4	1	1	3	0	2

Find:

a the mean number of letters delivered

_____

b the modal number of letters delivered

_____

c the median number of letters delivered.

_____

45 The table shows the number of workers in a factory who were absent during the first two weeks of August.

Number of days absent	0	1	2	3	4	5	6	7	8	9	10
Frequency	33	4	1	1	3	5	0	2	0	0	1

Find:

a the mean _____

b the mode _____

c the median. _____

1 Which temperature is higher?

  a 5° or 3°   _____

  b −5° or −3°   _____

  c −7° or −6°   _____

  d 4° or −4°   _____

2 Which temperature is higher?

  a −8° or −5°   _____

  b −4° or 4°   _____

  c −3° or −6°   _____

3 Which temperature is lower?

  a 7° or 6°   _____

  b −4° or −5°   _____

  c −2° or −4°   _____

  d 9° or 12°   _____

  e −1° or 1°   _____

4 Which temperature is lower?

  a −6° or −5°   _____

  b 4° or −5°   _____

  c −5° or −8°   _____

In questions **5** to **10**, use positive or negative numbers to describe the quantities.

5 **a** Ten seconds before the start of a race. _____

  b Ten seconds after the start of a race. _____

  c Going up a flight of 14 stairs. _____

  d The bottom of a pool that is 50 m below where you are standing. _____

  e A debt of $25. _____

6 Five minutes before the bus arrives. _____

7 Spending $100 in a shop. _____

8 Walking up a flight of ten steps. _____

9 Running 200 m back to school. _____

10 Falling 5 m from the branch of a tree. _____

11 Write either > or < between the two numbers.

  a 5   4   **b** −3   −1

  c −4   −8   **d** −3   −5

12 Write either > or < between the two numbers.

  a 7   8   **b** −5   −7

  c −3   −4   **d** −8   −7

In questions **13** and **14**, down the next two numbers in each sequence:

13 **a** −6, −3, 0,   _____

    b 12, 7, 2,   _____

    c −3, −6, −12,   _____

    d −8, −5, −2,   _____

14 **a** 5, 1, −3,   _____

    b −1, −4, −7,   _____

    c −10, −1, 8,   _____

    d −8, −4, 0,   _____

15 Find (use a number line if it helps):

  a 7 − 9   _____

  b −4 + 7   _____

  c (+3) − (+6)   _____

  d (+2) − (+6) + (+7) _____

  e (−7) − (+4) + (+5) _____

16 At 6 a.m. the temperature was −6°. By 9 a.m. it had risen by 4°.

  What was the temperature at 9 a.m.?   _____

17 Find (use a number line if it helps):

a $4 - 8$ _____

b $-7 + 6$ _____

c $(+5) - (+8)$ _____

d $(+3) - (+5) + (3)$ _____

e $(-5) - (+7) + (+4)$ _____

18 Find:

a $6 + (-7)$ _____

b $3 + (-8)$ _____

c $-5 - (-9)$ _____

d $-6 + (-6)$ _____

e $(-2) + (-2) + (-2)$ _____

f $10 + (-8) - (-4)$ _____

g $7 - (-6) + (-4)$ _____

In questions **19** to **23**, write the next two numbers in the sequence.

19 $5, -3, -11,$ _____

20 $-3, -6, -9,$ _____

21 $-2, -6, -18,$ _____

22 $2, 0, -2,$ _____

23 $-9, -3, -1,$ _____

24 **a** Subtract 9 from -4 _____

b Add $(+5)$ to (-6) _____

c Find the sum of $-4, -4$ and -5 _____

d Subtract positive 4 from negative 8 _____

25 **a** Subtract 3 from -3 _____

b Add -4 to -5 _____

c Subtract -5 from -4 _____

26 Find the difference between the sum of -4 and 3 and the sum of -8 and 5.

_____

27 Find:

a $(-12) \div (-4)$ _____

b $(-20) \div 5$ _____

c $-\dfrac{18}{6}$ _____

d $-\dfrac{30}{5}$ _____

28 Find:

a $(-8) \div 2$ _____

b $(-12) \div (-3)$ _____

c $\dfrac{-15}{3}$ _____

d $\dfrac{-45}{-15}$ _____

29 Calculate:

a $(-4) \times (+6)$ _____

b $(-3) \times (-5)$ _____

c $5 \times (-7)$ _____

d $-(-6)$ _____

e $-3(-5)$ _____

f $(-3) \times (-6)$ _____

g $(-6) \times (-2)$ _____

h $(+8) \times (-3)$ _____

30 Calculate:

a $(-4) \times (-6)$ _____

b $(-5) \times (-3)$ _____

c $(-7) \times (-5)$ _____

d $-(-9)$ _____

e $(-3) \times (-8)$ _____

f $(-10) \times (-6)$ _____

g $(-4) \times (-9)$ _____

h $(-2) \times (-3)$ _____

31 Find:

a $5 + (-3) - (-4)$ _____

b $7 + (-2) - (-7)$ _____

c $4 + (-3) - (-4)$ _____

d $7 + (-7) - (5)$ _____

e $-10 + (-8) - (-9)$ _____

f $9 + (-4) - (-2)$ _____

32 Find:

a $(5 - 9) - 3$ _____

b $(3 - 4) - (5 - 7)$ _____

c $(7 - 9) - 6$ _____

d $(8 - 3) - (10 - 8)$ _____

e $(6 - 12) - (7 - 4)$ _____

f $(10 - 9) - 5$ _____

33 **a** Subtract 5 from -8 _____

b Find the sum of -6 and $+9$ _____

c Subtract positive 4 from negative 8 _____

d Find the value of three times negative 6

_____

e Subtract (-4) from 4 _____

f Find the sum of -5 and -4 and -3 _____

34 Evaluate:

a $(-4) \times (-5)$ _____

b $(+2) \times (-7)$ _____

c $(-8) \times (-9)$ _____

d $(+6) \times (+3)$ _____

e $(-3) \times (-4)$ _____

f $-(-5)$ _____

g $6(-5)$ _____

35 Calculate:

a $-8 \div 4$ _____

b $18 \div (-6)$ _____

c $-36 \div -12$ _____

d $3 \div (-3)$ _____

e $(-4) \div (-8)$ _____

f $-3 \div 3$ _____

36 Calculate:

a $\dfrac{20}{-5}$ _____

b $\dfrac{12}{-4}$ _____

c $\dfrac{-60}{45}$ _____

d $\dfrac{-24}{-6}$ _____

e $\dfrac{-48}{-8}$ _____

37 Calculate:

a $12 - 4 \times (-2)$ _____

b $-6 \div 2(9 - 3)$ _____

c $5 \times (-2) - 7 \times (-3)$ _____

d $4 - 5 \div 2(7 - 4)$ _____

e $2(10 - 7) \div 3(5 - 3)$ _____

f $4(3 - 7) + 5(9 - 7)$ _____

g $3(7 + 3) \div 5 \times (-3)$ _____

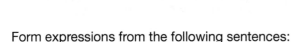

Form expressions from the following sentences:

1 Think of a number and add 10.

_____

2 Think of a number and subtract 4.

_____

3 The number 9 is subtracted from another number.

_____

4 A number is trebled.

_____

5 14 is multiplied by an unknown number.

_____

6 Simplify:

a $3x + 2 + 4x + 7$ _____

b $3x - 2 + 4x + 7$ _____

c $3x - 2 + 4x - 7$ _____

d $4x + 7 - 3x - 2$ _____

e $7x + 4y + 3x + 2y$ _____

7 Simplify:

a $7x + 4y - 3x + 2y$ _____

b $7x + 4y - 3x - 2y$ _____

c $7x + 4y + 3x - 2y$ _____

d $3x + 5y + 4z - x - 3y - 2z$ _____

e $2x - 3y + z + 3x + 3y + 2z$ _____

8 Simplify:

a $5x + x + 3x - 6x$ _____

b $4 - 3x - 7 + 4x$ _____

c $9 - 3 - 5 - 1$ _____

d $7x - 4x - 3x$ _____

9 Simplify:

a $5x + 4y - 3x + 7y$ _____

b $5x + 4y - 3x - 7y$ _____

c $5x - 4y + 3x + 7y$ _____

d $5x - 4y + 3x - 7y$ _____

10 Simplify:

a $4x + 5y + 6x + 2y + 3x + 4y$ _____

b $7x + 3y + 4x + 4y + 5x + 5y$ _____

c $3x + 2y + 2x + 7y + 6x + 3y$ _____

d $2x + 5y + 8x + y + 7x + 6y$ _____

11 Simplify:

a $3x + 5y - 5x + 2y + 6x - 2y$ _____

b $6x + 3y + 8x + 4y - 8x - 6y$ _____

c $4x + 2y - 2x + 7y + 5x + 9y$ _____

d $9x + 5y + 4x + 3y - 7x + 2y$ _____

12 Simplify:

a $8(2x + 3)$ _____

b $3(5 + 2a)$ _____

c $5(3x + 6)$ _____

d $7(6x + 4)$ _____

13 Simplify:

a $5x + 3(2x + 2)$ _____

b $3x + (4x + 3)$ _____

c $7x + 2(x + 4)$ _____

d $8x + 3(2x + 5)$ _____

14 Simplify:

  a $4(x + 1)$ _____

  b $5(2x + 1)$ _____

  c $3(4x + 2)$ _____

  d $2(5x + 4)$ _____

  e $3(7x + 3)$ _____

  f $10(4 + 3x)$ _____

  g $3(8x + 5)$ _____

15 Simplify:

  a $3 + 4(x + 2)$ _____

  b $5(2x + 1) + 4$ _____

  c $6 + 3(4x + 3)$ _____

  d $4x + 2(2x + 5)$ _____

  e $7 + 3(3x + 2)$ _____

  f $1 + 5(x + 3)$ _____

  g $3(x + 1) + 9$ _____

  h $6(3 + 2x) + 3x$ _____

  i $4(2 + 3x) + x$ _____

  j $5x + 2(4x + 1)$ _____

16 Write the following expressions in index form:

  a $a \times a \times a$ _____

  b $b \times b \times b \times b \times b$ _____

  c $z \times z$ _____

  d $c \times c \times c \times c$ _____

  e $x \times x \times x \times x \times x \times x \times x \times x \times x \times x \times x \times x \times x$ _____

  f $y \times y \times y \times y \times y$ _____

17 Write the following expressions in index form:

  a $p \times p \times p \times p$ _____

  b $z \times z \times z$ _____

  c $y \times y \times y \times y \times y$ _____

  d $p \times p \times p \times p \times p \times p \times p$ _____

18 Give the meanings of the following expressions (the first one is done for you):

  a y^3 $y^3 = y \times y \times y$

  b x^4 _____

  c z^5 _____

  d b^2 _____

  e c^6 _____

  f a^4 _____

19 Give the meanings of the following expressions:

  a y^4 _____

  b z^3 _____

  c a^7 _____

  d q^5 _____

20 Simplify:

  a $7 \times p$ _____

  b $4 \times c \times 5$ _____

  c $3a \times 2b \times a$ _____

  d $4 \times a \times b \times a \times b$ _____

21 Simplify:

  a $5 \times a$ _____

  b $4 \times x \times x \times x \times x$ _____

  c $2 \times a \times 7$ _____

  d $3 \times a \times b \times b \times b$ _____

  e $6 \times x \times y \times x \times y$ _____

  f $2 \times a \times a \times a \times b \times b$ _____

22 Write each expression in full without using indices:

  a $6x^2y$ _____

  b $5ab^2$ _____

c $3xyz$ _____

d $2p^3q^4$ _____

23 Write each expression without using indices:

a $4a^2$ _____

b $3xy^2$ _____

c $5x^2y^2$ _____

d $3xyz^2$ _____

e $4ab^3$ _____

f $3a^2b$ _____

g $6x^3yz^2$ _____

h $8pq^2r^3$ _____

24 Simplify the following expressions:

a $2a \times 4b$ _____

b $a^2 \times 6a$ _____

c $2a \times 3a \times 4a$ _____

d $3x \times 2y \times 4x$ _____

e $4b^2 \times 3b$ _____

f $a \times b \times 2a \times b$ _____

g $a^3 \times a$ _____

h $z^2 \times z \times 3z$ _____

i $2b \times 3b^2 \times b$ _____

25 Simplify the following fractions:

a $\dfrac{5}{7} \times \dfrac{14}{5}$ _____

b $\dfrac{3}{4} \times \dfrac{8}{9}$ _____

c $\dfrac{2}{3} \times \dfrac{12}{5}$ _____

d $\dfrac{a}{3} \times \dfrac{12}{a}$ _____

e $\dfrac{x}{3} \times \dfrac{5}{x}$ _____

f $\dfrac{4p}{3} \times \dfrac{15}{2p}$ _____

g $\dfrac{15b}{4} \times \dfrac{b}{3}$ _____

h $\dfrac{3a}{7} \times \dfrac{7}{6a}$ _____

i $\dfrac{3x}{4} \times \dfrac{8x}{7}$ _____

26 Simplify the following fractions:

a $\dfrac{2}{3} \div \dfrac{1}{6}$ _____

b $\dfrac{5}{9} \div \dfrac{2}{3}$ _____

c $\dfrac{x}{12} \div \dfrac{x}{3}$ _____

d $\dfrac{a}{2} \div \dfrac{a}{6}$ _____

e $\dfrac{2ab}{c} \div \dfrac{b}{3c}$ _____

f $\dfrac{6t}{7} \div \dfrac{3}{2t}$ _____

g $\dfrac{12}{a} \div \dfrac{6}{a}$ _____

h $\dfrac{7ab}{10} \div \dfrac{10a}{7}$ _____

i $\dfrac{9}{x} \div \dfrac{12}{x^2}$ _____

27 Simplify the following fractions:

a $\dfrac{a}{4} \div \dfrac{a}{8}$ _____

b $\dfrac{8b}{3} \div \dfrac{5b}{12}$ _____

c $\dfrac{pq}{qr} \div \dfrac{qs}{st}$ _____

d $\dfrac{8}{x} \div \dfrac{4}{x^2}$ _____

e $\dfrac{6p}{5} \div \dfrac{3p}{2}$ _____

f $\dfrac{12z}{25} \div \dfrac{3z^2}{5}$ _____

g $\dfrac{9a^2}{4} \div \dfrac{8}{3a}$ _____

h $\dfrac{5}{x} \div \dfrac{25}{x^2}$ _____

28 Find the value of $10 + 2x$ when:

a $x = 3$ _____

b $x = -3$ _____

c $x = 7$ _____

29 Find the value of $10 - 2x$ when:

a $x = 3$ _____

b $x = -3$ _____

c $x = 7$ _____

30 Find the value of $3p^2$ when:

a $p = 2$ _____

b $p = -2$ _____

c $p = -5$ _____

31 Find the value of $8 - 2q^2$ when:

a $q = -2$ _____

b $q = 1$ _____

c $q = 3$ _____

32 Find the value of x^3 when:

a $x = 3$ _____

b $x = -3$ _____

c $x = \dfrac{3}{2}$ _____

33 Find the value of $\frac{2x}{3} - \frac{5}{6}$ when $x = 2$.

_____

34 Find the value of $5xy$ when $x = 3$, $y = 5$.

_____

35 Find the value of $n(1 - 2n)$ when $n = -3$.

_____

36 Find the value of $2n(n - 1)$ when $n = 3$.

_____

37 Find the value of $\frac{p}{2}(p - q)$ when $p = 6$, $q = 2$.

_____

38 Find the value of $\frac{p^2}{4}$ when $p = 4$.

_____

39 Find the value of $b^2 - 4ac$ when $a = 4$, $b = 6$, $c = 2$.

_____

40 Find the value of $4a(3b - 4c)$ when $a = 5$, $b = 6$, $c = 7$.

_____

41 Find the value of $\frac{1}{2}(a + b + c)$ when $a = 5$, $b = 6$, $c = 7$.

_____

42 Find the value of $\frac{p^2 - pq}{11}$ when $p = 5$, $q = -6$.

_____

43 Find the value of $2(3x + 7) - 3(5 - 3y)$ when $x = 4$ and $y = -2$.

_____

44 Find the value of $5(2 - 4x) + 7(2y + 4) - 6z$ when $x = 3$, $y = -3$ and $z = -12$.

_____

In questions **45** to **47**, form an expression from the sentence.

45 'I think of a number, double it and subtract 4.'

_____

46 'I think of a number, multiply it by 4 and subtract 8.'

_____

47 Beverly had 20 golf balls and lost x of them. Her sister Alicia, had 15 golf balls and won y more golf balls. At the end of the day the two sisters put all their golf balls into one bag. Write an expression for the number of golf balls in the bag.

_____

48 Simplify $3(5x + 2) + 2(2 + 3x) + 4(5x + 1)$

_____

49 Simplify $2(2x + 1) - 3(x - 4) + 4(3x - 2)$

_____

50 Simplify $5(1 - 3x) - 2(4x - 3) + 3(5x - 3)$

_____

51 Simplify $4(2 - 5x) + 7(x - 5) - 3(3 - 6x)$

_____

In questions **1** to **9**, find the size of each angle marked with a letter.

1

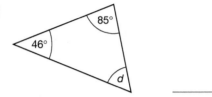

_____

2

_____

3

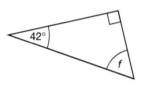

_____

4

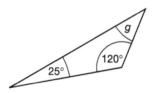

_____

5

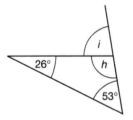

_____

_____

6

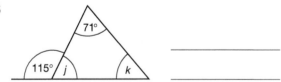

_____

_____

7

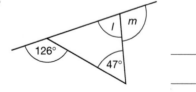

_____

8

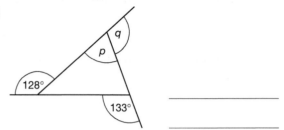

_____

_____

9

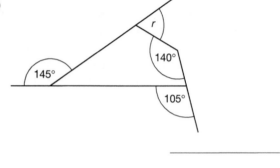

_____

_____

In questions **10** to **21**, you should carry out the constructions outside of your workbook.

In questions **10** to **12**, use the given data to construct the triangle. Calculate the third angle in each triangle and check the accuracy of your construction.

10 △ABC in which AB = 7 cm, ∠A = 30° and ∠B = 50°.

11 △DEF in which DF = 6 cm, ∠D = 90° and ∠F = 35°.

12 △PQR in which PR = 9 cm, ∠P = 40° and ∠R = 50°.

In questions **13** to **15**, use the given data to construct the triangle.

13 △ABC in which AB = 6 cm, AC = 8 cm and BC = 10 cm.

14 △DEF in which DF = 8.2 cm, DE = 4 cm and EF = 5.3 cm.

15 △PQR in which PR = 7.3 cm, PQ = 3.8 cm and QR = 7.3 cm.

In questions **16** to **21**, use the given data to construct the triangle. Draw a rough diagram first and then decide which method you will use. Where appropriate measure the third side.

16 △ABC in which AB = 6.5 cm, A = ∠50° and AC = 7.5 cm.

17 △DEF in which DF = 10 cm, DE = 7 cm and ∠D = 45°.

18 △PQR in which PR = 6.8 cm, ∠P = 63° and PQ = 5.7 cm.

19 △XYZ in which XY = 7.4 cm, ∠X = 78° and ∠Z = 48°.

20 △KLM in which KM = 4.5 cm, KL = 5.2 cm and LM = 8.3 cm.

21 △BCD in which BD = 5.3 cm, CD = 4.8 cm and ∠D = 66°.

In questions **22** and **23**, find the size of each angle marked with a letter.

22

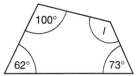

$l =$ _____

23

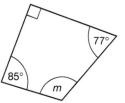

$m =$ _____

24 Find the equal angles n.

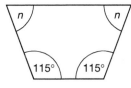

$n =$ _____

25 The angle p is half the angle q. Find angles p and q.

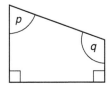

$p =$ _____

$q =$ _____

26 Angles r and s are supplementary. Find the angles r, s, t and u.

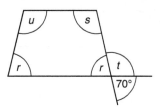

$r =$ _____

$s =$ _____

$t =$ _____

$u =$ _____

In questions **27** to **36**, find the size of each angle marked with a letter.

27

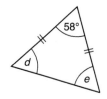

_____

_____

28

_____

_____

_____

29

_____

_____

30

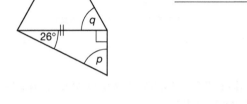

_____

_____

_____

36

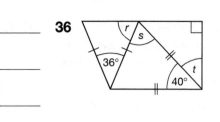

_____

_____

_____

_____

In questions **37** to **40**, make accurate drawings of the quadrilaterals.

_____

In each case measure all the angles in the quadrilateral and find their sum.

_____

Is your value what you expected?

31

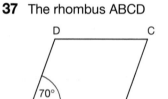

37 The rhombus ABCD

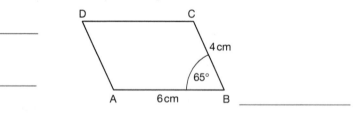

_____

32

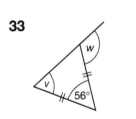

_____

_____

38 The parallelogram ABCD

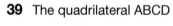

_____

_____

_____

33

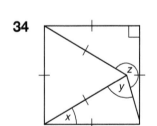

_____

_____

39 The quadrilateral ABCD

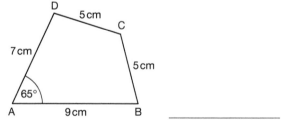

34

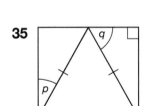

_____

_____

_____

_____

40 The trapezium PQRS

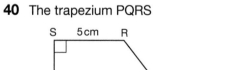

35

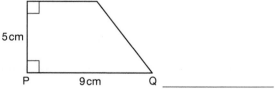

_____

_____

Review test 2: units 8 to 13

In questions **1** to **20**, choose the letter that gives the correct answer.

1 Written as a decimal $\frac{7}{10} + \frac{3}{1000}$ is:

   A 0.73   **B** 0.703

   C 0.0703   **D** 0.073

2 $0.4 \times 0.7 =$

   A 0.0028   **B** 0.028

   C 0.28   **D** 2.8

3 $5.93 \div 4$, correct to three decimal places, is:

   A 1.48   **B** 1.482

   C 1.483   **D** 1.4825

4 $0.4^2 =$

   A 0.00016   **B** 0.0016

   C 0.016   **D** 0.16

5 9.30857 correct to three decimal places is:

   A 9.308   **B** 9.3086

   C 9.309   **D** 9.31

6 $0.5 \div 25 =$

   A 0.002   **B** 0.02

   C 0.2   **D** 2

7 $0.0034 \times 1000 =$

   A 340   **B** 34

   C 3.4   **D** 0.34

8 $2.22 - 0.3 - 1.02 =$

   A 0.72   **B** 0.9

   C 1.5   **D** 2.94

9 The temperatures of two objects are −7° and −4°. The difference between these temperatures is:

   A 11°   **B** 7°

   C 4°   **D** 3°

10 The temperature of a solid is −3°. If its temperature is lowered by 5° its new temperature will be:

   A −5°   **B** −7°

   C −8°   **D** 2°

11 At 4 o'clock the obtuse angle between the hands of a clock is:

   A 90°   **B** 120°

   C 150°   **D** 210°

12 Each angle in an equilateral triangle is:

   A 45°   **B** 50°

   C 60°   **D** 90°

13 Three angles of a quadrilateral are 55°, 75° and 115°. The remaining angle is:

   A 85°   **B** 95°

   C 105°   **D** 115°

14 Which of the following statements are true?

   i Vertically opposite angles are equal.

   ii 120° and 80° are supplementary angles.

   iii 70° and 20° are complementary angles.

   A i and ii only   **B** ii and iii only

   C none of these   **D** i and iii only

15

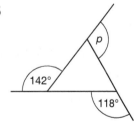

The size of the angle p is:

   A 38°   **B** 62°

   C 90°   **D** 100°

Questions **16** to **19** refer to the figure below.

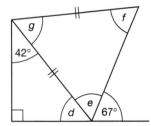

16 The size of the angle *d*, in degrees, is:

    A 42°   **B** 48°

    C 52°   **D** 58°

17 The size of the angle *e*, in degrees, is:

    A 42°   **B** 48°

    C 65°   **D** 85°

18 The size of the angle *f*, in degrees, is:

    A 42°   **B** 48°

    C 65°   **D** 85°

19 The size of the angle *g*, in degrees, is:

    A 42°   **B** 48°

    C 50°   **D** 65°

20 Look at the following statements.

    i Vertically opposite angles are supplementary.

    ii The four angles of a quadrilateral add up to 360°.

    iii The complement of 40° is 60°.

    iv The opposite angles of a rhombus are equal.

    Which statements are false?

    A i and ii   **B** iii and iv

    C ii and iii   **D** none of these

21 Write as fractions:

    a 0.65   _____

    b 0.61   _____

    c 0.008   _____

    d 0.042   _____

22 Write the following numbers as decimals:

    a $\dfrac{11}{100}$ _____

    b $\dfrac{67}{100}$ _____

    c $5\frac{7}{8}$ _____

    d $7\frac{29}{100}$ _____

23 Find:

    a 0.46 + 0.046   _____

    b 7.32 + 6.71   _____

    c 5.04 + 0.07   _____

    d 6.72 + 1.008   _____

24 Find:

    a 12.5 – 3.6   _____

    b 43.9 – 6.88   _____

    c 104.8 – 67.03 _____

    d 0.06 – 0.0084 _____

25 Find:

    a 4.9 – 3.7 + 6.7 _____

    b 2.4 – 0.24 + 2.4 _____

    c 67 – 7.92 – 4.82 _____

    d 16.4 – 8.93 + 6.79 _____

26 Find the cost of 32 articles costing $53.30 each.

    _____

27 The perimeter of a regular pentagon is 48.5 cm. Calculate the length of one side.

    _____

28 Give 83.5057 correct to:

    a the nearest whole number _____

    b two decimal places   _____

    c three decimal places.   _____

29 Give each number correct to the nearest whole number:

a 27.4 _____

b 5.5945 _____

c 43.055 _____

30 Give the following numbers correct to three decimal places:

a 2.742 67 _____

b 83.8326 _____

c 51.0606 _____

31 Give the following numbers correct to the number of decimal places indicated in brackets:

a 0.25 (1) _____

b 0.0745 (2) _____

c 6.345 34 (3) _____

d 16.9278 (2) _____

32 Calculate, giving your answers correct to two decimal places:

a 0.466 ÷ 6 _____

b 37.7 ÷ 9 _____

c 83.92 ÷ 7 _____

33 Calculate, giving your answers correct to one decimal place:

a 943 ÷ 6 _____

b 623 ÷ 4 _____

c 519 ÷ 17 _____

34 Calculate, giving your answers correct to three decimal places:

a 7.41 ÷ 4 _____

b 0.038 ÷ 8 _____

c 5.276 ÷ 13 _____

35 Give these fractions as exact decimals:

a $\frac{7}{8}$ _____ **b** $\frac{9}{16}$ _____ **c** $\frac{7}{40}$ _____

36 Find the exact answers for these questions:

a 0.048 ÷ 0.6 _____

b 0.03 ÷ 0.006 _____

c 18.72 ÷ 5.2 _____

37 Find the exact answers for these questions:

a 0.63 × 0.3 _____

b 5.26 × 0.8 _____

c 9.6 × 0.6 _____

38 Calculate, giving your answer correct to the number of decimal places in the brackets:

a 6.785 ÷ 8 (2) _____

b 43 ÷ 11 (4) _____

c 0.54 ÷ 2.6 (3) _____

d 0.0072 ÷ 0.063 (3) _____

39 The dress sizes of a group of women were recorded as:

12 10 14 14 12 16 10 10 18 14

12 14 8 16 16 14 14 12 18 14

16 14 14 12 10 16 14 10 10 18

12 8 14 16 12 10 14 12 16 8

14 12 16 12 18 10 14 16 10 12

12 16 16 14 16 14 16 10 14 18

Complete this frequency table.

Dress size	Tally	Frequency
8		
10		
12		
14		
16		
18		

40 This bar chart shows how the pupils in Year 1 at Breswell Secondary School travelled to school on a particular day.

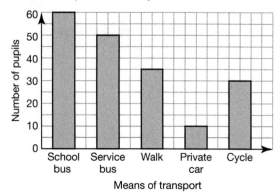

a What was the most common way of coming to school?

_____

b What was the least common way of coming to school?

_____

c What transport was used by exactly 30 pupils?

_____

d How many Year 1 pupils attended school on this particular day?

_____

e How many pupils did not come, either on the school bus or the service bus?

_____

41 The table shows the gold medals awarded to the top five countries in the 2012 Summer Olympics.

Country	USA	China	Great Britain	Russia	S Korea
Number of gold medals	46	38	29	20	13

On a separate piece of paper, show these on a bar chart.

42 Find the median of each of the following sets:

a 23 19 15 11 9

_____

b 34 3 26 32 42 45 49 34

_____

c 2.68 2.72 2.67 2.58 2.74 2.66

_____

43 For the set of numbers
81 94 82 78 92 78 80 79 83 find:

a the mean   _____

b the mode   _____

c the median   _____

44 Which temperature is the higher?

a −6° or 3°   _____

b −8° or −3°   _____

c −9° or −11°   _____

45 Which temperature is the lower?

a −4° or 5°   _____

b −9° or −5°   _____

c −12° or −11°   _____

46 Write either > or < between the two numbers:

a 9   6   **b** −4   −6

c 3   −7   **d** −9   −3

47 Write the next two numbers in the sequence:

a 9, 4, −1, _____

b 10, 5, 0, _____

c −3, −10, −17, _____

48 Find:

   a $5 - 10$ _____

   b $-6 - 3$ _____

   c $(+3) - (+6)$ _____

   d $(-3) + (-5) + (+12)$ _____

49 Find:

   a $9 + (-4) - (-6)$ _____

   b $(-4) + (-7) - (-15)$ _____

   c $(-12) - (-5) - (-10)$ _____

   d $(20) - (-4) + (-12)$ _____

50 a Subtract 7 from -6 _____

   b Subtract -3 from -5 _____

   c Add -7 to -2 _____

51 Multiply out the following brackets:

   a $(-6) \times (-2)$ _____

   b $(-5) \times (-8)$ _____

   c $(-2) \times (-3)$ _____

   d $(-3) \times (-4) \times (-5)$ _____

52 Find:

   a $(-16) \div 4$ _____

   b $(-16) \div (-4)$ _____

   c $\dfrac{-24}{8}$ _____

   d $\dfrac{-27}{-9}$ _____

53 a Subtract positive 3 from negative 3.

   _____

   b Find the sum of -5 and -10.

   _____

   c Find the value of four times negative 4.

   _____

   d Find the sum of -7, -9 and 18.

   _____

54 Calculate:

   a $19 - 2 \times (-5) + 11$ _____

   b $(-12) \div 4 + 2(6 - 4)$ _____

   c $5(8 - 4) + 5(7 - 3)$ _____

   d $4(9 - 3) \div 3(11 - 2)$ _____

55 Simplify:

   a $7x - 3x + 4x - 2$ _____

   b $5 + 2x - 3 - 5$ _____

   c $12 - 7 - 2 - 3$ _____

   d $8 + 5x - 5 - 2x$ _____

56 Simplify:

   a $12x + 5y - 9x + 2y$ _____

   b $9x - 2y + 3x - 2y$ _____

   c $8x + 5x - 3y + 6y$ _____

   d $10x - 3x - 4x + 2y$ _____

57 Simplify:

   a $5x + 2x - 3y - 5y + 2x + 7y$ _____

   b $3x + 5y + 4x - y - 5x + 2y$ _____

   c $7x - 3x + 10y - 3y + 4x - y$ _____

   d $x + 2x - 5y + 2y + 7x - 3y$ _____

58 Simplify:

   a $3(4x - 2)$ _____

   b $5(2 - 3a)$ _____

   c $7(5 + 3b)$ _____

   d $4(3x - 4)$ _____

59 Simplify:

  a $4x + 3(2x - 3)$ _____

  b $7x + (5 - 4x)$ _____

  c $8x - 2(2x - 4)$ _____

  d $5x - 3(4x - 2)$ _____

60 Write the following expressions in index form:

  a $a \times a \times a \times a$ _____

  b $c \times c \times c$ _____

  c $p \times p \times p \times p \times p \times p$ _____

  d $a \times a \times a \times b \times b$ _____

61 Give the meanings of the following expressions (the first one is done for you):

  a p^3 $p^3 = p \times p \times p$ _____

  b q^4 _____

  c r^2 _____

  d s^5 _____

62 Simplify:

  a $5 \times a$ _____

  b $2 \times b \times b$ _____

  c $7 \times a \times b \times a \times b$ _____

  d $3 \times a \times b \times b \times b$ _____

63 Write each expression without using indices:

  a $4a^2b$ _____

  b $5ab^2$ _____

  c $7abc^2$ _____

  d $9a^2bc^2$ _____

64 Simplify the following expressions:

  a $5x \times 2y \times 2x$ _____

  b $2 \times b \times 3$ _____

  c $3a \times 5b \times 4a$ _____

  d $6x \times 3y \times 2x \times y \times 4z$ _____

65 Simplify $5(3x - 2) + 3(2x + 1) + 4(5x - 3)$

_____

66 Simplify $2(4x - 1) + 3(x - 2) + 4(3x - 5)$

_____

67 Simplify $7(2x - 3) + 2(3x - 4) - 3(4x - 1)$

_____

68 Simplify $4(5x - 2) - 5(2x + 1) + 6(5x - 2)$

_____

69 Simplify $3(3x - 5) - 2(5x + 2) + 3(7x - 4)$

_____

70 Find the value of $3xy$ when $x = 4$ and $y = 7$

_____

71 Find the value of $4(3x - 2) + 2(2x + 5) - (6x - 1)$ when $x = 5$

_____

72 Find the value of $4(2x + 3) + 2(3x - 5) - 3(4x - 4)$ when $x = -3$

_____

73 Find the value of $x(3x - 1)$ when:

  a $x = 4$ _____

  b $x = -4$ _____

74 Find the value of $5(2x - 1)$ when:

  a $x = 3$ _____

  b $x = 5$ _____

In questions **75** to **78**, find the size of each angle marked with a letter:

75

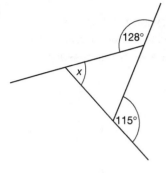

_____

76

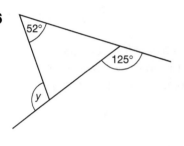

_____

77

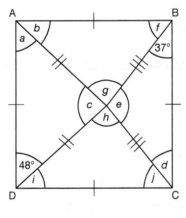

_____

_____

_____

_____

_____

_____

78

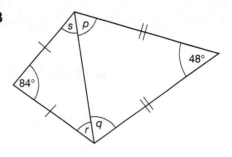

_____

_____

_____

_____

In questions **79** and **80**, make accurate drawings of each quadrilateral. In each case, measure all four angles and find their sum. Is your value what you expected?

79 The rhombus ABCD.

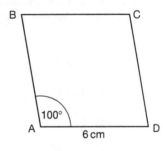

_____

80 The quadrilateral ABCD.

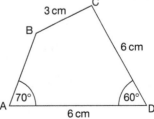

_____

1 Express each percentage as a fraction in its lowest terms:

a 40% _____   **g** $66\frac{2}{3}$% _____

b 60% _____   **h** $82\frac{1}{2}$% _____

c 45% _____   **i** $12\frac{1}{2}$% _____

d 20% _____   **j** $10\frac{2}{3}$% _____

e 54% _____   **k** 180% _____

f 72% _____   **l** 250% _____

2 Express each percentage as a fraction in its lowest terms:

a 48% _____   **d** $15\frac{1}{2}$% _____

b 75% _____   **e** $8\frac{1}{3}$% _____

c 35% _____   **f** 175% _____

3 Express the following percentages in decimals giving answers correct to three decimal places where necessary:

a 53% _____   **e** $41\frac{2}{3}$% _____

b 18% _____   **f** $14\frac{2}{3}$% _____

c 155% _____   **g** $3\frac{1}{3}$% _____

d $37\frac{3}{4}$% _____   **h** $42\frac{4}{7}$% _____

4 Express the following percentages as decimals giving answers correct to three decimal places where necessary:

a 45% _____   **d** $5\frac{2}{3}$% _____

b 125% _____   **e** $54\frac{2}{3}$% _____

c $7\frac{3}{4}$% _____   **f** $68\frac{2}{7}$% _____

5 Express the following fractions as percentages, giving answers correct to one decimal place where necessary:

a $\frac{1}{4}$ _____   **e** $\frac{5}{8}$ _____

b $\frac{9}{10}$ _____   **f** $\frac{43}{60}$ _____

c $\frac{17}{20}$ _____   **g** $\frac{33}{25}$ _____

d $\frac{23}{40}$ _____   **h** $\frac{8}{7}$ _____

6 Express the following fractions as percentages, giving answers correct to one decimal place where necessary:

a $\frac{5}{9}$ _____   **d** $\frac{31}{65}$ _____

b $\frac{18}{25}$ _____   **e** $\frac{12}{7}$ _____

c $\frac{29}{40}$ _____   **f** $\frac{9}{8}$ _____

7 Express the following decimals as percentages:

a 0.75 _____   **e** 0.535 _____

b 0.44 _____   **f** 0.005 _____

c 0.38 _____   **g** 0.175 _____

d 1.64 _____   **h** 5.421 _____

8 Express the following decimals as percentages:

a 0.55 _____   **d** 0.735 _____

b 0.27 _____   **e** 0.006 _____

c 1.83 _____   **f** 4.215 _____

9 Complete the following table:

Fraction	Percentage	Decimal
$3\frac{1}{2}$		
	40%	
		0.85
$\frac{7}{40}$		
	64%	
		0.24

10 Complete the following table:

Fraction	Percentage	Decimal
$7\frac{1}{2}$		
	30%	
		0.65
$\frac{9}{40}$		
	46%	
		0.84

11 If 83% of the students in a school have a cell phone, what percentage do not have one?

12 In a class 37% of the students study metalwork. What percentage do not study metalwork?

13 If 76% of the cost of a litre of gas is tax, what percentage is the actual cost of the gas?

14 A cricket team won 55% of their matches and drew 12%. What percentage did they lose?

15 In a basketball league the winning team drew 12.5% of their matches and lost 5%. What percentage of their matches did they win?

16 In a school 43% of the pupils study Spanish and 39% study French. If 13% study both languages what percentage do not study either language?

17 Joe spends 45% of his income on household expenses, 27% on pleasure, saves 6%, and spends the remainder on his car. What percentage does Joe spend on his car?

18 An object is 47% animal, 31% vegetable and the remainder is mineral. What percentage of the object is mineral?

19 The cost of running a car is 26% fuel, 30% road tax, insurance and repairs, and the remainder depreciation. What percentage accounts for depreciation?

20 Deductions from Eli's wages amount to 40% of her earnings. What are her deductions when she earns $960?

21 A make of jam contains 45% fruit, 38% sugar and the remainder is water. Find the percentage of the jam that is water.

22 Express the first quantity as a percentage of the second.

a 4, 40 _____

b 50, 75 _____

c 12 cm, 60 cm _____

d 243 mm, 30 cm _____

e 1400 g, 2 kg _____

f 2.64 kg, 8.8 kg _____

g 5 ft, 20 ft _____

h 4 pints, 5 pints _____

i 65 cm, 2 m _____

j 850 m, 2 km _____

k 66 cm², 99 cm² _____

l 3 yd, 9 yd _____

m 83c, $2 _____

23 Express the first quantity as a percentage of the second.

a 6, 80 _____

b 27, 45 _____

c 243 g, 900 g _____

d 396 km, 1320 km _____

e 80 cm, 5 m _____

f 8 litres, 10 litres _____

g $4.98, $12 _____

h 2040 m, 6 km _____

24 Express the second quantity as a percentage of the first.

a 10 cm, 4 cm _____

b 5 pints, 3 pints _____

c 1.2 m, 28 cm _____

d 2 litres, 844 cm³ _____

e 450 g, $157\frac{1}{2}$ g _____

f 1 t, 750 kg _____

g 20, 60 _____

h 60, 20 _____

i 25, 50 _____

j 10 litres, 12 litres _____

k 74 cm, 18.5 mm _____

l 8.5 t, 1.87 t _____

m $56, 336c _____

25 Express the second quantity as a percentage of the first.

a 30, 28 _____

b 5 litres, 1.7 litres _____

c 550 g, 352 g _____

d 40, 80 _____

e 30 m, 36 m _____

f 80, 40 _____

g $296, 740c _____

h 34 cm, 221 mm _____

26 Find the value of:

a 30% of 6 m _____

b 65% of 5 kg _____

c 55% of 460 cm² _____

d 76% of 1350 km _____

e 32% of 450 mm² _____

f 96% of 55 000 _____

g 85% of 2.5 km _____

h $12\frac{1}{2}$% of 720 m _____

i $66\frac{2}{3}$% of 336 g _____

j $37\frac{1}{2}$% of 16 litres _____

k $5\frac{1}{4}$% of $5600 _____

l $33\frac{1}{3}$% of $66 _____

m $\frac{3}{4}$% of $2000 _____

27 Find:

a 40% of 600 g _____

b 35% of $4440 _____

c 16% of $35 500 _____

d 55% of 840 cm² _____

e 84% of 6500 cm _____

f 26% of 1250 km _____

g $33\frac{1}{3}$% of 96 litres _____

h 0.25 % of 1440 km _____

28 In a history test Arlene scored 26 out of 40.

What percentage is this? _____

29 In a class of thirty-six, 75% of the students are boys.

a How many boys are there? _____

b How many girls are there in the class?

_____

30 In a population of 12 500, fifty-five per cent are males. What percentage are females?

_____

31 Express 50% as a fraction. _____
If 50% of a number is 30, what is the number?

_____

32 Express 20% as a fraction. _____
If 20% of a number is 13 find the number.

_____

33 Express 60% as a fraction. _____
If 60% of a sum of money is $9.84 find the sum of money.

_____

34 In an election 40% voted for Fisher, 35% voted for Morgan and 15% voted for Pigeon. If 2500 people were entitled to vote how many:

a voted for Fisher _____

b voted for Pigeon _____

c failed to vote? _____

35 On a particular day, of the 600 workers in a factory, $3\frac{1}{2}$% were absent due to illness. How many of the employees were ill?

_____

36 A piece of frozen fish lost 4% of its mass when thawed. If its mass was 1.92 kg when thawed, what was its mass when frozen?

_____

37 In a sale an article was marked down from $268 to $174.20. Find:

a the reduction in dollars _____

b the reduction as a percentage of the

original price. _____

38 A shopkeeper reduces his prices by 30c in the $.

a What percentage was this? _____

b What was the reduction on an article

marked $760? _____

39 A textbook has 350 pages of which 30% have pictures, 10% have tables and 6% have both tables and pictures. How many pages have:

a pictures _____

b only tables _____

c just plain text? _____

40 Last year Barbados received 472 000 tourists. 29% of these came from the UK, 26% from the USA and 12% from Canada.
How many tourists:

a came from Canada _____

b came from the UK _____

c came from a country other than the three

countries named above? _____

41 The religious persuasion of the people living in St Vincent and the Grenadines is: Anglican 42%, Roman Catholic 19%, Methodist 20%, other 19%. If 111 000 live on these islands how many are:

a Anglican _____

b Methodist _____

c neither Anglican nor Roman Catholic?

_____

42 The annual cost of insuring a motorbike is 7% of its purchase price. I paid $4600 for my motorbike. How much will it cost to insure it for:

a one year _____

b three years? _____

43 In the end of term exams Peggy scored 704 out of a possible 800.

a What percentage was this? _____

b How many more marks would Peggy have needed to get 90% of the available marks?

_____

44 A packet of cereal was full when it left the factory but 'settling' caused the volume taken by the cereal to be reduced by 8%. If its original volume was 3000 cm^3, find the volume taken by the cereal after it had settled.

_____

45 In an auction, Joe sells a piece of furniture for $755. The auctioneer deducts 12% of the sale price as his commission.

a Work out the commission. _____

b How much does Joe get for his piece of

furniture? _____

46 Sabina bought a coat in a sale. It was originally marked $250 but she managed to get a reduction of 40%.

a How much was the reduction?

_____

b Express the price she paid for it as a percentage of the marked price.

_____

47 In a family, 40% are males. What is the smallest number of females in the family?

_____

48 In a school 55% are girls and 108 are boys. How many girls are there?

_____

49 Esther bought a calculator for $20. She sold it at a loss of 40%.

   a What percentage of the price she paid for the calculator did Esther sell it for?

   _____

   b How much did she sell it for?

   _____

50 A shopkeeper bought 300 articles for $12 000 and sold them at $35 each. Find:

   a his total income from the sale

   _____

   b his profit

   _____

   c his profit as a percentage of the price he paid for them.

   _____

15 Units of measurement

1 Express the given quantity in terms of the unit in brackets:

a 7 m (cm) _____

b 12 km (m) _____

c 24 cm (mm) _____

d 56 km (cm) _____

e 7.4 m (cm) _____

f 6.2 m (mm) _____

g 3.4 cm (mm) _____

h 0.44 km (m) _____

2 Express the given quantity in terms of the unit in brackets:

a 4 kg (g) _____

b 15 t (kg) _____

c 40 g (mg) _____

d 3.5 t (kg) _____

e 0.4 g (mg) _____

f 1.8 kg (g) _____

g 0.7 g (mg) _____

h 0.8 kg (mg) _____

3 Express the given quantity in terms of the unit in brackets:

a 1 m 40 cm (cm) _____

b 5 cm 8 mm (mm) _____

c 6 m 55 cm (cm) _____

d 2 km 750 m (m) _____

e 7 g 500 mg (mg) _____

f 2 t 750 kg (kg) _____

g 4 kg 200 g (g) _____

h 1 kg 350 mg (mg) _____

4 Express the given quantity in terms of the unit in brackets:

a 700 mm (cm) _____

b 14 cm (m) _____

c 3450 m (km) _____

d 4 600 000 mm (km) _____

e 650 g (kg) _____

f 2200 mg (g) _____

g 2500 kg (t) _____

h 750 mg (g) _____

5 Express the given quantity in terms of the unit in brackets:

a 2 m 75 cm (cm) _____

b 7 km 40 m (km) _____

c 6 cm 8 mm (cm) _____

d 10 m 45 cm (m) _____

e 3 kg 443 g (kg) _____

f 7 kg 55 g (kg) _____

g 4 kg 89 g (g) _____

h 8 g 750 mg (mg) _____

6 Express the given quantity in terms of the unit in brackets:

a 7 m + 56 cm (m) _____

b 460 m + 3 km (km) _____

c 6 cm + 8 mm (cm) _____

d 550 mm + 46 cm + 2 m (m) _____

e 2 m + 34 cm (mm) _____

f 26 cm + 56 mm + 1 m (mm) _____

g 2.8 km + 290 m (m) _____

h 2 m + 39 cm + 600 mm (cm) _____

7 Express the given result in terms of the unit in brackets:

a 3 t + 735 kg (kg) _____

b 7 kg + 450 g (kg) _____

c 44 kg + 0.3 t + 60 kg (kg) _____

d 2.8 t + 56 kg (kg) _____

e 3 m – 78 cm (cm) _____

f 2.4 m – 845 mm (cm) _____

g 2.5 t – 774 kg (kg) _____

h 4.6 kg – 845 g (g) _____

8 Express:

a 3.4 m in centimetres _____

b 56 g in milligrams _____

c 0.04 kg in grams _____

d 3 cm 7 mm in millimetres _____

e 0.045 km in metres _____

f 3 km 500 m in metres _____

g 3 kg 350 g in grams _____

h 3 t 475 kg in kilograms _____

9 Express:

a 650 mm in centimetres _____

b 14 cm 5 mm in millimetres _____

c 5 km 65 m in kilometres _____

d 8 kg 321 g in kilograms _____

e 7650 m in kilometres _____

f 5 g 350 mg in milligrams _____

g 0.075 km in metres _____

h 0.05 km in centimetres _____

10 Express :

a 5 m + 74 cm in metres _____

b 245 m + 4 km in kilometres _____

c 470 mm + 45 cm + 3 m in metres _____

d 65 mm + 4 cm + 1 m in metres _____

e 2 t + 495 kg in tonnes _____

f 7.3 kg – 743 g in kilograms _____

g 64 kg + 0.6 t + 195 kg in kilograms _____

h 6.4 m – 665 mm in centimetres _____

11 Calculate, giving your answer in the unit given in brackets:

a 5 × 2 kg 420 g (g) _____

b 7 × 3 m 44 cm (m) _____

c 3 × 5 km 340 m (km) _____

d 8 × 4 kg 750 g (kg) _____

e 4 × 4 km 540 m (m) _____

f 9 × 8 m 56 cm (cm) _____

12 The length of one side of a square is 5.4 cm. Find the perimeter of the square in millimetres.

_____

13 Find, in metres, the perimeter of a rectangle in which the lengths of adjacent sides are 2.37 m and 560 cm.

_____

14 Find the total mass, in kilograms, of 750 g of mixed fruit, 675 g of flour and 460 g of butter.

_____

15 Keith started part-time work last Monday, 5 July. He works every morning and is due to get his first pay at the end of his tenth complete working day.

a On what date will he get his first pay?

_____

b What day of the week is this?

_____

16 Write 200 minutes in hours and minutes.

_____

17 Write 250 hours in days and hours.

_____

18 An evening steel pan concert began at 7.30 p.m. and concluded at 9.10 p.m. If there was a 20-minute interval, for how long was the band playing?

_____

19 Novelia's cookbook says that for the meat she is about to cook she should allow 25 minutes per 500 g plus 20 minutes extra. How long should it take to cook a $3\frac{1}{2}$ kg piece of meat?

_____

20 A programme starts at 11.50 a.m. and finishes at 1.25 p.m. Kelly has a DVD with 1 hour 30 minutes free time remaining on it. Is this long enough for her to record the whole programme?

_____

21 Ed and Maud Anjers went to a concert which was due to begin at 7.30 p.m. They kept careful details of the timings. The first item lasted 13 minutes; the second item lasted 30 minutes; the third item lasted 62 minutes.

They were in their seats by 7.20 p.m. The concert started 3 minutes late. There was a 3-minute break between the first two items and a 20-minute interval after the second item. The third item overran by 2 minutes.

What time did the concert end?

_____

22 Write the unit that would be the most sensible to measure:

a the mass of a tablet of soap _____

b the length of a truck _____

c the distance between Trinidad and

Barbados _____

d the time it takes to fly in a jet from Kingston

to New York. _____

23 A field has four sides. The lengths of three of the sides are 58 m, 136 m and 205 m. If the perimeter of the field is 536 m, find the length of the fourth side.

_____

24 Nabez went to watch a cricket match. As soon as the match finished he went home. He took 13 minutes to walk to the bus stop, where he waited for 7 minutes before the bus arrived. The bus ride took 35 minutes and he had a 12-minute walk before he reached home at 1933. What time did the match finish?

_____

25 Given below is a typical timetable for John's working day.

7.10	Get up
7.25	Leave home
7.55	Arrive at work (5 minutes early)
10.20 – 10.30	Morning break
12.30 – 1.00	Lunch break
2.50 – 3.00	Afternoon break
5.00	Finish work
5.35	Arrive home
6.30 – 7.00	Main meal
8.30	Go out
11.30	Return home
11.45	Go to bed

a How long is it from the time John gets up until he is due to start work?

_____

b How long is it from the time he gets up until he goes to bed? _____

c How long is he at home after work before he goes out? _____

d What is the length of his working day:

   i including breaks

   _____

   ii excluding breaks?

   _____

e How much longer does he work in the morning than in the afternoon?

_____

f How much sleep does he normally get from one working day to the next?

_____

26 Express the given quantity in the unit in brackets:

a 8 yd 2 ft (ft)   _____

b 3 ft 4 in (in)   _____

c 1 mile 500 yd (yd)   _____

d 5 ft 7 in (in)   _____

27 Express the given quantity in the unit(s) in brackets:

a 48 in (ft)   _____

b 50 in (ft and in)   _____

c 15 ft (yd)   _____

d 70 ft (yd and ft)   _____

28 Express the given quantity in the unit(s) in brackets:

a 3 lb 8 oz (oz)   _____

b 2 tons 5 cwt (cwt)   _____

c 63 oz (lb and oz)   _____

d 160 lb (cwt and lb)   _____

29 Write the first unit roughly in terms of the unit in brackets:

a 4 kg (lb)   _____

b 10 lb (kg)   _____

c 50 miles (kilometres)   _____

d 200 km (miles)   _____

30 Which is heavier:

   a a 6 lb of carrots or a 4 kg bag of carrots

_____

   b a 20 kg bag, or a 56 lb bag of cement?

_____

31 Which is the larger page size:

240 mm × 165 mm or 10 in × 7 in?

_____

32 The instructions for repotting a plant say that it should go in a 20 cm pot. The flower pots I have are marked 5 in, 8 in and 10 in. Which one should I use?

_____

33

33 ft

21 ft

What, roughly, are the dimensions of this rectangle in metres?

_____

For questions **34** to **39**, use the estimate that 1 metre ≈ 39 inches

34 How much longer or shorter is 200 metres than 220 yards? Give your answer correct to the nearest 50 inches. (Tip: convert each distance into inches.)

_____

35 Estimate the number of yards in a 1500 m race.

_____

36 Estimate the number of metres in one mile.

_____

37 Roughly, how much further is it to walk a mile than 1500 metres?

_____

38 An athlete in training runs 200 laps around a 400 metre track. He estimates that he has run about 5 miles. Is he correct? Justify your answer.

_____

39 In Rugby Union football, the distances between the try line and the nearest line across the width of the field, was known as the '25'. It was so-called because, when imperial measurements were used the distance was 25 yards.

Today the equivalent line is known as the '22'. This is because the distance between the two lines after the change was 22 metres. Which line was nearer to the try line:

   a the 25 yard line, when the measurements were in imperial units

   b the 22 metre line after distances had changed to metric measurements?

Work out each distance in inches before giving your answer.

_____

1 For each figure, draw the axis of symmetry.

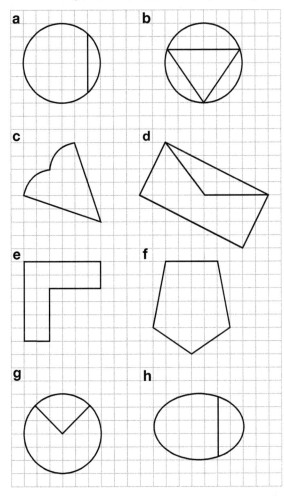

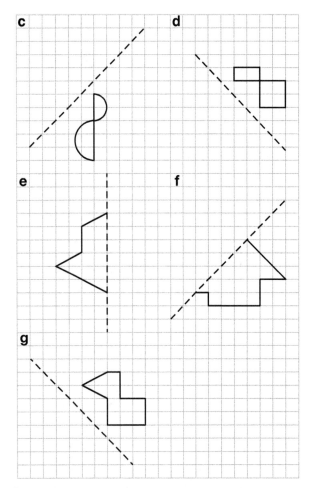

2 Complete the following drawings so that each broken line is an axis of symmetry.

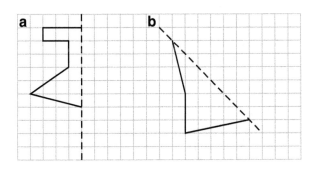

3 For each figure draw the two axes of symmetry.

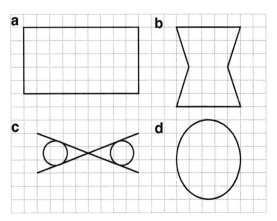

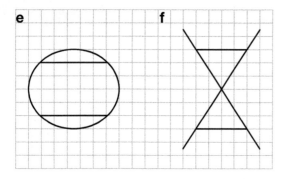

4 Complete the following drawings so that each broken line is an axis of symmetry.

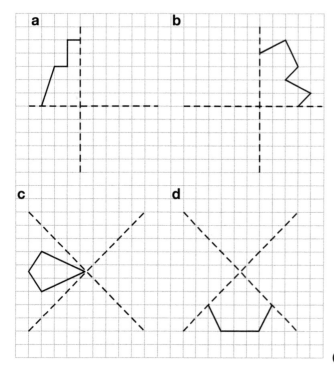

5 Complete the following drawings so that each broken line is an axis of symmetry.

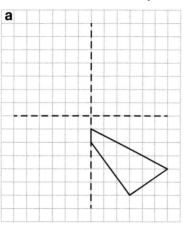

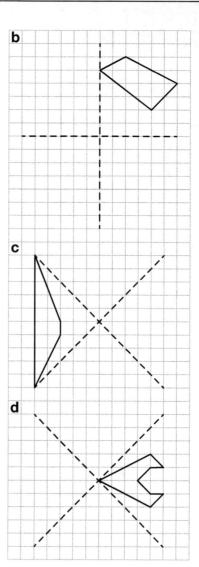

6 Draw the axes of symmetry for these shapes. Some have more than one.

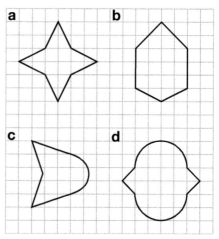

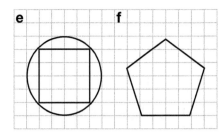

7 How many axes of symmetry are there for each of the following shapes?

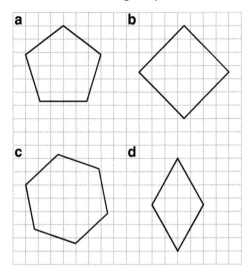

8 Which of these shapes have rotational symmetry? _____

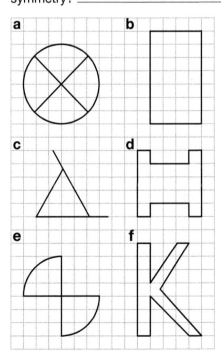

In questions **9** to **12**, complete the drawing so that the broken lines are axes of symmetry.

9

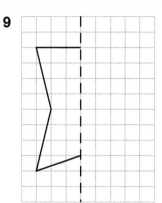

10

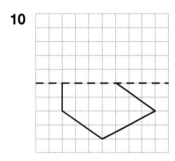

11

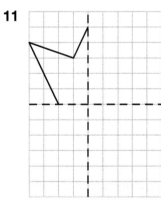

12

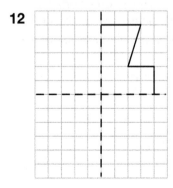

In questions **13** to **15**, draw the reflection of each object in the mirror line.

13

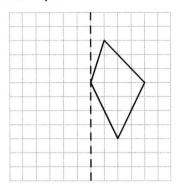

14

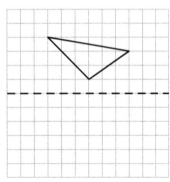

15

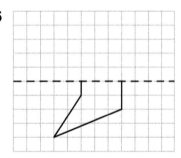

In questions **16** to **19**, draw the reflection of the given object in the mirror line. In questions **16** to **18**, the vertices of the object are labelled A, B, C, etc. Label the corresponding images of the vertices A′, B′, C′, etc.

16

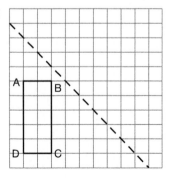

17

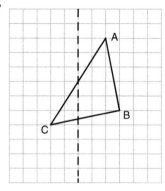

18

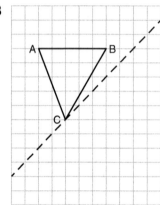

19

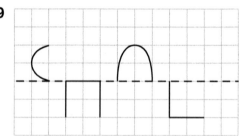

20 Draw the mirror image of each object.

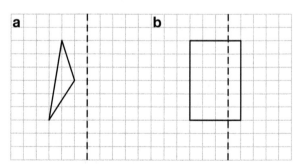

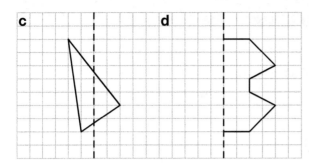

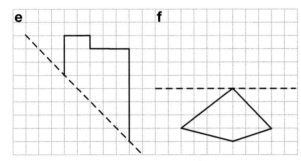

21 For each of the following images (A, B, C etc) and mirror images (A′, B′, C′ etc), draw in the mirror line.

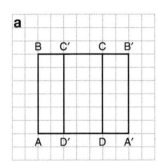

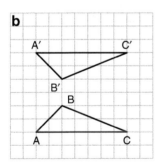

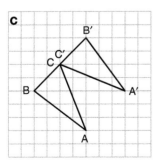

22 Draw the mirror lines.

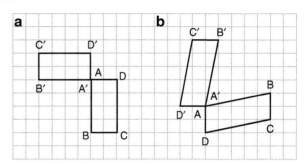

23 On the grid below, draw sketches to illustrate the following translations:

a An object is translated 4 cm to the right.

b An object is translated 5 units parallel to an east–west line, to the right.

c An object is translated 3 m due south.

d An object is translated 4 km north.

e An object is translated 3 units parallel to a north–south line, upwards.

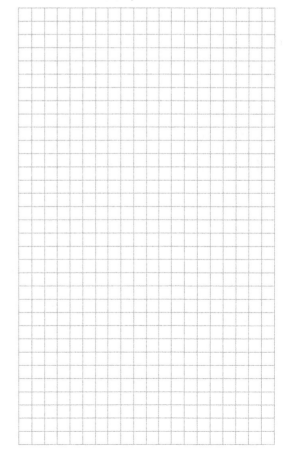

In questions **1** to **12**, count squares to find the area of each shape.

1

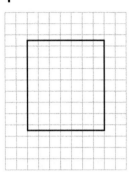

_____

2

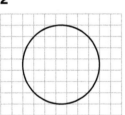

_____

3

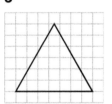

_____

4

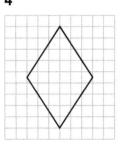

_____

5

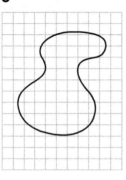

_____

6

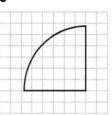

_____

7

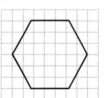

_____

8

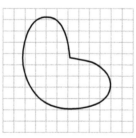

_____

9

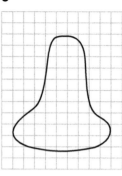

_____

10

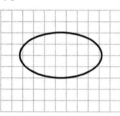

_____

11

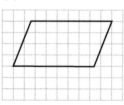

_____

12

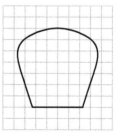

_____

Find the area of each of the following shapes, clearly stating the units of your answer:

13 A square of side 7 cm.

_____

14 A square of side 2.6 m.

_____

15 A rectangle measuring 9 cm by 12 cm.

_____

16 A rectangle with adjacent sides 3.6 cm and 4.8 cm.

_____

17 A square of side 56 km.

_____

18 A rectangle measuring 1.7 m by 2.6 m.

_____

19 A square of side 0.45 m.

_____

20 A rectangle measuring 50 mm by 34 mm.

_____

Find the area of each of the following rectangles. Give your answer in the unit in brackets.

21 A rectangle measuring 55 mm by 7 cm. (cm^2)

_____

22 A rectangle measuring 45 mm by 6 cm. (mm^2)

_____

23 A rectangle measuring 34 mm by 4.5 cm. (cm^2)

_____

24 A rectangle measuring 450 cm by 7 m. (m^2)

_____

In questions **25** to **32**, each shape is made from rectangles. For each shape find:

a its perimeter

b its area.

In questions **25** to **30**, the measurements are given in centimetres.

25

a _____

b _____

26

a _____

b _____

27

a _____

b _____

28

a _____

b _____

29

a _____

b _____

30

a _____

b _____

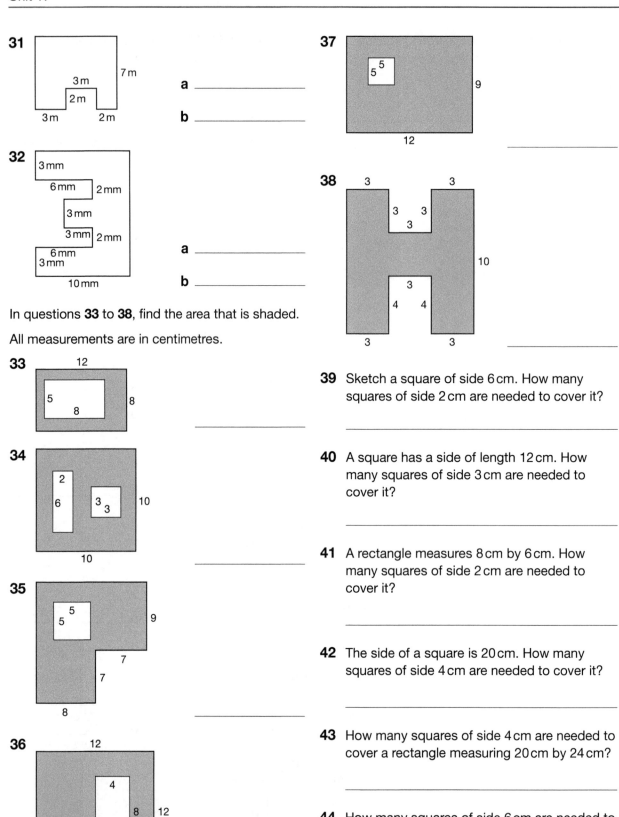

31

7 m
3 m
2 m
3 m   2 m

a _____

b _____

32

3 mm
6 mm   2 mm
3 mm
3 mm   2 mm
6 mm
3 mm
10 mm

a _____

b _____

In questions **33** to **38**, find the area that is shaded.

All measurements are in centimetres.

33

12
5
8
8
8

_____

34

2
6
3 3
10
10

_____

35

5
5
9
7
7
8

_____

36

12
4
8   12
12

_____

37

5
5
9
12

_____

38

3   3
3   3
3
10
3
4   4
3   3

_____

39 Sketch a square of side 6 cm. How many squares of side 2 cm are needed to cover it?

_____

40 A square has a side of length 12 cm. How many squares of side 3 cm are needed to cover it?

_____

41 A rectangle measures 8 cm by 6 cm. How many squares of side 2 cm are needed to cover it?

_____

42 The side of a square is 20 cm. How many squares of side 4 cm are needed to cover it?

_____

43 How many squares of side 4 cm are needed to cover a rectangle measuring 20 cm by 24 cm?

_____

44 How many squares of side 6 cm are needed to cover a rectangle measuring 42 cm by 36 cm?

_____

45 Express in cm²:

  a 0.07 m²   _____

  b 0.55 m²   _____

  c $6\frac{1}{2}$ m²   _____

46 Express in mm²:

  a 8 m²   _____

  b 5500 cm²   _____

47 Express in m²:

  a 7500 cm²   _____

  b 450 000 cm²   _____

48 Express in km²:

  a 890 000 m²   _____

  b 23 000 000 cm²   _____

49 Express in cm²:

  a 60 mm²   _____

  b 0.035 m²   _____

  c 95 000 mm²   _____

50 Express:

  a 0.35 m² in cm²   _____

  b 2 m² in mm²   _____

  c 5200 cm² in m²   _____

  d 450 000 m² in km²   _____

  e 760 000 mm² in cm²   _____

  f 270 cm² in mm²   _____

51 This table gives some of the measurements for various rectangles. Fill in the missing values.

Length	Breadth	Perimeter	Area
7 cm		24 cm	
12 cm		36 cm	
	4 m	26 m	
	5 m	28 m	
8 cm			32 cm²
12 m			84 m²
	14 mm		280 mm²
44 cm			1452 cm²

In questions **52** to **59**, find the area of each of the rectangles, giving your answer in the unit given:

	Length	Breadth	
52	5 m	0.3 m	_____ cm²
53	70 mm	4.5 cm	_____ mm²
54	0.8 m	0.6 m	_____ cm²
55	800 cm	500 cm	_____ m²
56	$2\frac{1}{2}$ m	$\frac{1}{2}$ m	_____ cm²
57	3.5 cm	2.4 cm	_____ mm²
58	340 m	250 m	_____ km²
59	56 cm	65 mm	_____ cm²

In questions **60** to **63** find:

  a the area of the surface

  b the perimeter of the surface.

60 A square board for playing draughts or chess with side 32 cm.

  a _____

  b _____

61 A hockey pitch measuring 57 m by 91 m.

   a _____

   b _____

62 A football pitch measuring 110 yd by 60 yd.

   a _____

   b _____

63 A pool table measuring 1.83 m by 3.66 m.

   a _____

   b _____

64 A roll of paper is 22 cm wide and 5 m long. Find:

   a its area in cm^2

    _____

   b its perimeter when unrolled, in cm

    _____

   c its area in m^2

    _____

65 How many square tiles, of side 15 cm are needed to cover a wall measuring 3.9 m by 2.4 m?

    _____

66 My rectangular bathroom measures 2.1 m by 1.95 m. The rectangular area covered by the bath measures 190 cm by 75 cm and the pedestal for the hand basin covers $200\,cm^2$.

   Work out:

   a the perimeter of the bathroom

    _____ m

   b the floor area of the bathroom

    _____ m^2

   c the area of floor-covering needed

    _____ m^2.

67 Clive wants to tile a wall 4 m wide and 2.4 m high with tiles measuring 15 cm by 20 cm. He would like the longer side of each tile to be vertical.

   a Can he do this without cutting any tiles?

    _____

   b How many tiles measuring 15 cm by 20 cm are needed to tile this wall if no tile is cut?

    _____

   c The tiles are sold in boxes, each holding 100 tiles. How many boxes must he buy?

    _____

68 A cricket pitch is 66 feet long and 12 feet wide. The distance between the batting creases is 58 feet.

   Find:

   a the area of the pitch in:

    i square feet

    _____

    ii square yards.

    _____

   b the area between the batting creases.

    _____

   c the perimeter of the pitch in:

    i feet

    _____

    ii yards.

    _____

Find the areas of the rectangles in questions **1** to **6**.

1

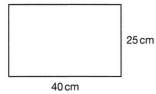

25 cm

40 cm

2

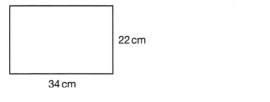

22 cm

34 cm

3

7.2 cm

18.5 cm

4 A rectangle measuring 0.7 cm by 0.6 cm.

5 A rectangle measuring $3\frac{1}{2}$ cm by $5\frac{3}{4}$ cm.

6 A rectangle of length 0.56 cm and width 0.35 cm.

Find the areas of the following shapes in square centimetres. All measurements are in centimetres.

7

3

3

3

4

8

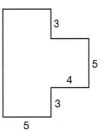

3

5

4

3

5

9

2

6

7

2

10

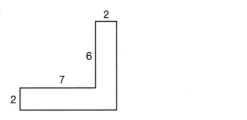

10

3

3

3

3

8

11

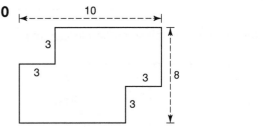

14

4

4

4

4

10

Find the areas of the following parallelograms:

12

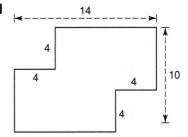

8 cm

9 cm

10 cm

13

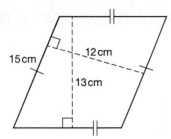

15 cm   12 cm

13 cm

18 $9\frac{1}{2}$ cm

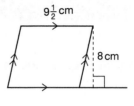

8 cm

14

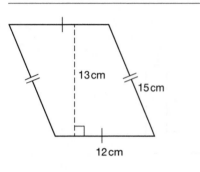

13 cm   15 cm

12 cm

19

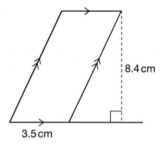

8.4 cm

3.5 cm

Find the areas of the following parallelograms:

15

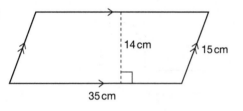

14 cm   15 cm

35 cm

20

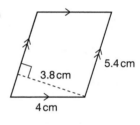

3.8 cm   5.4 cm

4 cm

16

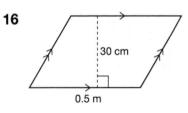

30 cm

0.5 m

21   5 cm

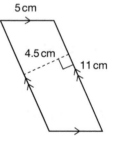

4.5 cm   11 cm

17

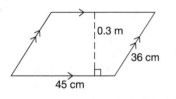

0.3 m

36 cm

45 cm

22

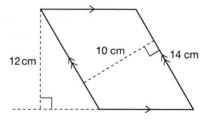

12 cm   10 cm   14 cm

23

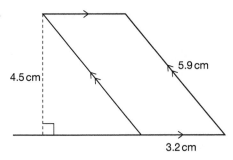

4.5 cm

5.9 cm

3.2 cm

24

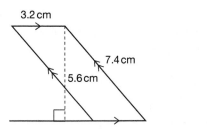

3.2 cm

7.4 cm

5.6 cm

In questions **25** to **35**, find the area of each of the triangles.

25

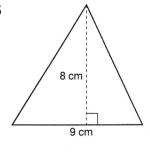

8 cm

9 cm

26

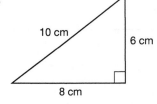

10 cm

6 cm

8 cm

27

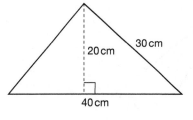

20 cm

30 cm

40 cm

28

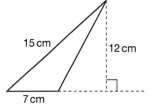

15 cm

12 cm

7 cm

29

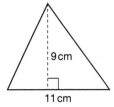

9 cm

11 cm

30

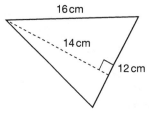

16 cm

14 cm

12 cm

31

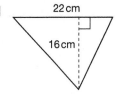

22 cm

16 cm

32

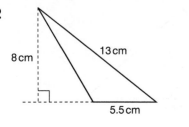

33

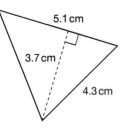

34

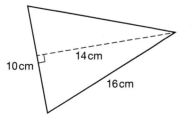

35

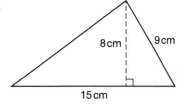

36 Find the area of this parallelogram.

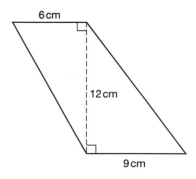

37 Find the missing measurements for the following triangles:

Area	Base	Height
18 cm²	9 cm	
60 cm²		8 cm
168 cm²		14 cm
42 cm²	12 cm	
120 cm²	16 cm	
81 cm²		9 cm

In questions **38** to **47**, find the area of the compound shapes.

38

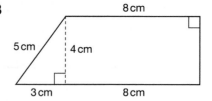

39

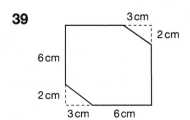

40

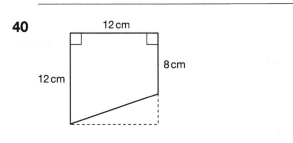

41

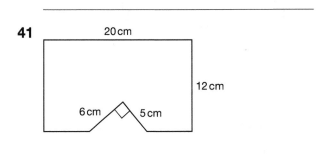

42

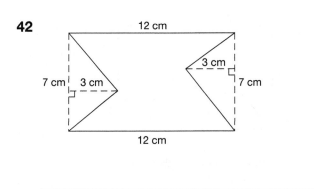

43

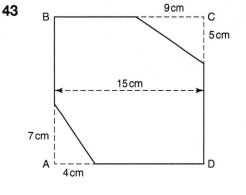

44

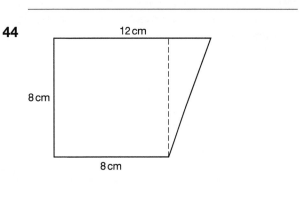

45

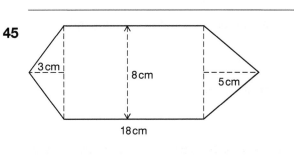

46

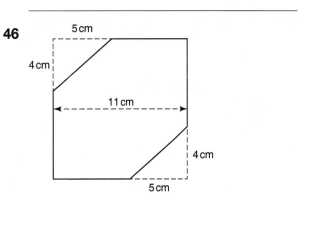

47

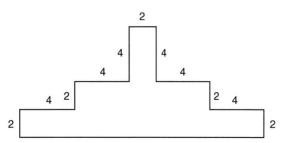

6.5 cm

9 cm

10.4 cm

Find the area of:

a the rectangle _____

b triangle A _____

c triangle B _____

d the strip between triangles A and B.

_____

48 The diagram shows the cross-section through the base of a monument. All measurements are in metres.

2

4 4

4 4

4 2 2 4

2 2

Find:

a the perimeter of the cross-section

_____

b its area.

_____

In questions **49** to **51**, all measurements are in centimetres.

49 A rectangle measuring 9 cm by 6 cm is to be divided into four pieces as shown in the diagram.

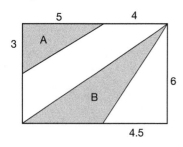

5 4

3

A

6

B

4.5

50 This rectangle is to be divided into five pieces as shown in the diagram.

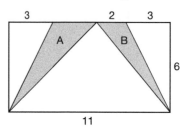

3 2 3

A B

6

11

Find the area of:

a the rectangle _____

b triangle A _____

c triangle B. _____

51 This rectangle is divided into four triangles.

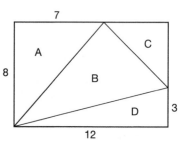

7

A C

8

B

D 3

12

Find the area of each triangle.

A _____

B _____

C _____

D _____

52 The diagram shows a rectangular flag with a cross.

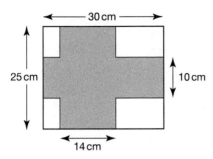

Find:

a the area of the shaded cross

_____

b the area that is white.

_____

53 This rectangle is divided into four triangles. All measurements are in centimetres.

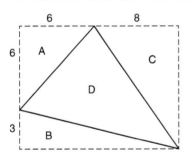

Find the area of each triangle.

A _____

B _____

C _____

D _____

54 Find the area of this triangle. All measurements are in centimetres.

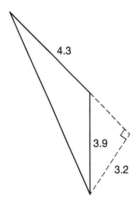

_____

19   Algebra 2

Form equations to illustrate the following statements and find the unknown numbers:

1 I think of a number, subtract 5 and get 7.

_____

2 I think of a number, add 2 and get 9.

_____

3 If a number is added to 7, we get 12.

_____

4 If a number is subtracted from 10, we get 6.

_____

5 I think of a number, double it and get 18.

_____

6 If a number is multiplied by 5, the result is 20.

_____

7 When we multiply a number by 3, we get 24.

_____

8 Five times an unknown number gives 35.

_____

9 Write sentences to show the meaning of the following equations:

a $4x = 12$ _____

b $x + 8 = 12$ _____

c $x - 5 = 1$ _____

d $x - 7 = 10$ _____

Solve the equations:

10 a $x + 5 = 15$ _____

b $7 + y = 9$ _____

c $a + 6 = 13$ _____

d $x + 3 = 15$ _____

e $a + 1 = 10$ _____

11 a $9 + c = 20$ _____

b $x + 2 = 4$ _____

c $x - 5 = 9$ _____

d $a - 3 = 1$ _____

e $y - 6 = 5$ _____

12 a $x - 4 = 0$ _____

b $c - 7 = 3$ _____

c $a - 1 = 2$ _____

d $t - 10 = 10$ _____

e $9 = x + 2$ _____

13 a $5 = x - 2$ _____

b $1 = a - 5$ _____

c $4 = c - 6$ _____

d $x - 3 = 10$ _____

e $7 = x + 1$ _____

14 a $7 = x - 1$ _____

b $a - 2 = 2$ _____

c $c - 9 = 9$ _____

d $1 = x - 4$ _____

Solve the equations:

15 a $5 = x + 4$ _____

 b $11 = a - 10$ _____

 c $11 = a + 10$ _____

 d $x - 8 = 4$ _____

16 a $4x = 20$ _____

 b $5b = 30$ _____

 c $3a = 15$ _____

 d $2x = 12$ _____

 e $7x = 14$ _____

17 a $8y = 8$ _____

 b $2a = 7$ _____

 c $7a = 2$ _____

 d $6x = 3$ _____

 e $x + 5 = 9$ _____

18 a $a - 4 = 7$ _____

 b $3x = 21$ _____

 c $9 = x - 3$ _____

 d $9 = a + 3$ _____

 e $5x = 4$ _____

19 a $a - 9 = 3$ _____

 b $12a = 6$ _____

 c $6a = 12$ _____

 d $10 = x + 7$ _____

 e $x - 7 = 10$ _____

20 a $5x + 3 = 13$ _____

 b $4x + 1 = 13$ _____

 c $3a - 2 = 19$ _____

 d $5x - 4 = 6$ _____

 e $53 = 8x - 3$ _____

21 a $25 = 2x + 1$ _____

 b $9x - 70 = 20$ _____

 c $8x + 2 = 50$ _____

 d $7x - 1 = 3$ _____

 e $4a + 3 = 6$ _____

22 a $3t - 4 = 3$ _____

 b $2x + 5 = 8$ _____

 c $5x - 6 = 14$ _____

 d $9z + 7 = 9$ _____

 e $6a + 7 = 11$ _____

23 a $5a + 3 = 7$ _____

 b $3x - 7 = 3$ _____

 c $2t + 7 = 8$ _____

 d $8x - 5 = 11$ _____

 e $4z + 7 = 9$ _____

 f $6a + 11 = 15$ _____

24 a $4x - 9 = 15$ _____

 b $15 = 7x + 4$ _____

 c $6a - 11 = 13$ _____

 d $5z + 3 = 19$ _____

 e $3m + 2 = 16$ _____

 f $9x - 17 = 4$ _____

Form equations to illustrate the following statements. Then solve them:

25 I think of a number, multiply it by 3 and subtract 5. The result is 10.
What was the number?

_____

26 I think of a number, multiply it by 5 and subtract 8. The result is 32.
What was the number?

_____

27 When 7 is added to an unknown number the result is 13. What is the number?

_____

28 I think of a number, multiply it by 4 and add the result to 8. The total is 44. What is the number?

_____

Solve the equations:

29 a $3x + 5 = 2x + 7$ _____

  b $5x - 3 = 2x + 6$ _____

  c $3x - 6 = x + 4$ _____

  d $7x + 4 = 5x + 8$ _____

  e $3x + 5 = 7x + 2$ _____

30 a $5 = 6x + 1 - 5x$ _____

  b $4x + 2 + x = 7$ _____

  c $2x - 7x + 6x = 9$ _____

  d $3x + 2 + 2x = 7$ _____

  e $7 - 3x - 4 + 6x = 18$ _____

31 a $7 + x + 2x = 3 + 5x$ _____

  b $1 + 7 - 6 + 3x = 4x$ _____

  c $5 - x + 3 + x = 2x$ _____

  d $5x - 3x + x = x + 6$ _____

  e $3x - 1 - x + 6 = 4x + 3$ _____

32 Simplify:

  a $4(x + 1)$ _____

  b $5(2x + 1)$ _____

  c $3(4x + 2)$ _____

  d $2(5x + 4)$ _____

  e $3(7x + 3)$ _____

  f $10(4 + 3x)$ _____

  g $3(8x + 5)$ _____

33 Simplify:

  a $3 + 4(x + 2)$ _____

  b $5(2x + 1) + 4$ _____

  c $6 + 3(4x + 3)$ _____

  d $4x + 2(2x + 5)$ _____

  e $7 + 3(3x + 2)$ _____

  f $1 + 5(x + 3)$ _____

  g $3(x + 1) + 9$ _____

  h $6(3 + 2x) + 3x$ _____

  i $4(2 + 3x) + x$ _____

  j $5x + 2(4x + 1)$ _____

34 Solve the equations:

  a $3(x + 1) = 12$ _____

  b $4(a + 1) = 16$ _____

  c $3(2b + 3) = 15$ _____

  d $9 + 3(x + 2) = 21$ _____

  e $4(x + 1) + 5 = 13$ _____

  f $3x + 4 = 4(2x + 1)$ _____

  g $4x - 3 = 2 + (2x + 1)$ _____

  h $2(x + 3) + 3 = 4x + 8$ _____

  i $5(x + 1) + 2 = 3x + 11$ _____

  j $7 + 4(2x + 1) = 10x + 3$ _____

35 Solve the equations:

  a $3 - (x - 6) = 4$ _____

  b $5 - (2x + 1) = 3$ _____

  c $4x - 3(x - 2) = 8$ _____

  d $x - 5(2 - x) = 2$ _____

  e $4(3 - x) - 2(4 - 3x) = 8$ _____

  f $5(2 - x) + 3(2x + 1) = 16$ _____

  g $2(x + 5) - 5(2x - 7) = 13$ _____

h $2(x - 3) + 3x - (2 - x) = 22$ _____

i $6(x - 2) - 2x - 3(x - 5) = 7$ _____

j $5(2x - 3) + 3x - (1 - 3x) = 8$ _____

36 Find a number such that when it is added to two-thirds of itself, the result is 50.

_____

37 The lengths of the three sides of a triangle are x cm, x cm and 7 cm. The perimeter is 35 cm. Find x.

_____

38 The three sides of a triangle have lengths $(x + 2)$ cm, $(x - 3)$ cm and $2x$ cm. The perimeter is 39 cm. Find x.

_____

39 Some 1 litre and $\frac{1}{2}$ litre bottles are filled with milk. If there are three times as many $\frac{1}{2}$ litre bottles as there are 1 litre bottles and the total amount of milk is 45 litres, how many $\frac{1}{2}$ litre bottles are there?

_____

40 The lengths of the sides of a quadrilateral are $(2x + 2)$ cm, $2x$ cm, $(3x + 1)$ cm and $(5x - 3)$ cm. If the perimeter of the quadrilateral is 48 cm, find the length of:

a the shortest side _____

b the longest side. _____

41 Find four consecutive whole numbers whose sum is 90. _____

42 John is three years older than Susan and Khalied is five years younger than her. The sum of their ages is 40. Find their ages.

_____

43 How do Maria and John share $100 if John receives $47 less than twice what Maria receives?

_____

44 Find two consecutive whole numbers such that when the greater number is added to twice the smaller number, the answer is 52.

_____

45 Find two consecutive odd numbers such that twice the greater number plus the smaller number gives an answer of 61.

_____

46 Find three consecutive whole numbers whose sum is 153.

_____

47 Find four consecutive whole numbers whose sum is 166.

_____

48 Find two consecutive even numbers such that the greater number plus three times the smaller number is 130.

_____

49 Amy and Beth are two sisters. The sum of their ages now is 31 years. Eight years ago Amy was twice as old as Beth. How old is each sister now?

_____

50 Mrs Korada is three times as old as her son Frank. Six years ago the sum of their ages was 36. What are their present ages?

_____

51 The mass of a cup is half as much again as the mass of a saucer and the mass of a plate is twice the mass of a saucer. If the total mass of five plates, six cups and nine saucers is 2.8 kg, find the mass, in grams, of:

a a saucer _____

b a plate _____

c a cup _____

d a cup, saucer and plate _____

52 Anita has 29c and Andres has 51c. How much must Anita give to Andres so that Andres has four times as much as Anita?

_____

53 In triangle ABC below, AB = BC and AC = 8 cm. The perimeter of the triangle is 26 cm.

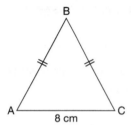

8 cm

a Find AB. _____

b What special name do we give to triangle

ABC? _____

54 I subtract 21 from five times a certain number. I then double the result. The answer is 18. Find the original number.

_____

55 Find two consecutive whole numbers such that the sum of five times the smaller and four times the larger is 121.

_____

56 The sum of two numbers is 20. Five times the smaller number is eight less than four times the larger number. Find the numbers.

_____

57 A shop has 59 cans of cola on its shelves when it opens for the day. During the morning it sells x cans and in the afternoon it sells twice as many cans as it did in the morning. If there are 35 cans on the shelves when it closes, how many cans were sold in the afternoon?

_____

58 Black pencils cost 10c each and coloured pencils cost 12c each. If a pack of 50 assorted pencils cost $5.60 how many of the pencils are:

a black _____

b coloured? _____

59 A large jug holds five times as more water than a small jug. When $\frac{1}{5}$ litre is poured from the large jug to the small jug, the large jug contains three times as much as the small jug. How much was in each jug to start?

_____

_____

60

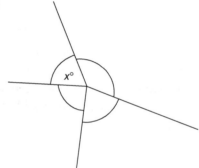

The smallest of four angles that meet at a point is $x°$. Compared with x, the other three angles are respectively twice as large as x, 20° greater than x, and 40° greater than x. Find x.

_____

_____

Write the next two terms in each of the following sequences:

1 1, 3, 5, 7, _____

2 4, 7, 10, 13, 16, _____

3 24, 12, 6, 3, _____

4 3, –4, –11, _____

5 0, 2, 6, 12, _____

6 12, –10, 8, –6, _____

7 19, 15, 11, 7, _____

8 The nth term of a sequence is $3n$.
Write the first three terms and the 10th term.

_____

9 The nth term of a sequence is $2n + 3$.
Write the first three terms and the 8th term.

_____

10 The nth term of a sequence is $15 - 2n$.
Write the first three terms and the 12th term.

_____

11 The nth term of a sequence is $8 + n$.
Write the first three terms and the 15th term.

_____

12 The nth term of a sequence is $2 - 2n$.
Write the first three terms and the 20th term.

_____

13 The nth term of a sequence is $3n + 7$.
Write the first three terms and the 30th term.

_____

14 The nth term of a sequence is $3n + 1$.
Write the first three terms and the 20th term.

_____

15 The nth term of a sequence is $4n - 2$.
Write the first three terms and the 15th term.

_____

In questions **16** to **20**, you are given the expression for the nth term and also one of the terms of the sequence. Check that the given term is correct, then write the first four terms and the tenth term.

16 nth term $= \dfrac{1}{2(n+1)}$, 10th term $= \dfrac{1}{22}$

_____

17 nth term $= \dfrac{1}{3n-2}$, 8th term $= \dfrac{1}{22}$

_____

18 nth term $= n + 7$, 12th term $= 19$

_____

19 nth term $= 7 + 2n$, 7th term $= 21$

_____

20 nth term $= 5n - 4$, 8th term $= 36$

_____

In questions **21** to **27**, find an expression for the nth term. Use your expression to check the terms that are given and write the next two terms in each sequence.

21

n	1	2	3	4	5	6
nth term	2	4	6	8		

_____

22

n	1	2	3	4	5	6
nth term	3	5	7	9		

_____

23

n	1	2	3	4	5	6
nth term	1	3	5	7		

24

n	1	2	3	4	5	6
nth term	0	1	2	3		

25

n	1	2	3	4	5	6
nth term	49	48	47	46		

26

n	1	2	3	4	5	6
nth term	0.6	0.3	0.2	0.15		

27

n	1	2	3	4	5	6
nth term	12	6	4	3		

In questions **28** to **31**, find an expression for the nth term. Check your expression by using it to find the first three terms.

28

n	1	2	3	4	5	6
nth term				12	15	18

29

n	1	2	3	4	5	6
nth term				18	27	38

30

n	1	2	3	4	5	6
nth term				18	21	24

31

n	1	2	3	4	5	6
nth term				24	35	48

32 The terms of a sequence are generated by starting with 4 and adding 3 each time.

   a Write the first five terms in a table like those given in questions **28** to **31**.

   b Find an expression for the nth term.

33 The terms of a sequence are generated by starting with 20 and subtracting 3 each time.

   a Write the first five terms in a table like those given in questions **28** to **31**.

   b Find an expression for the nth term.

34 The terms of a sequence are generated by doubling the position number and subtracting 1.

   a Write the first five terms in a table like those given in questions **28** to **31**.

   b Find an expression for the nth term.

35 The terms of a sequence are generated by adding 4 to twice the position number.

    a Write the first five terms in a table like those given in questions **28** to **31**.

    b Find an expression for the nth term.

    _____

36 The terms of a sequence are generated by subtracting 4 from the position number.

    a Write the first five terms in a table like those given in questions **28** to **31**.

    b Find an expression for the nth term.

    _____

In questions **37** to **42**, find an expression for the nth term and write the next three terms of the sequence.

37 4, 9, 14, 19, _____

_____

38 4, 8, 12, 16, _____

_____

39 $\dfrac{1}{3}, \dfrac{1}{6}, \dfrac{1}{9}, \dfrac{1}{12},$ _____

_____

40 5, 8, 11, 14, _____

_____

41 $1, \dfrac{1}{3}, \dfrac{1}{5}, \dfrac{1}{7},$ _____

42 500, 250, 125, 62.5, _____

_____

1 How many $100 bills are needed to pay for a chair costing $5300?

_____

2 How many $50 bills are needed to pay for a cell phone costing $830? How much change will there be?

_____

3 HB pencils are sold in packs of 8 or 12. The pack of 8 costs $7 while the pack of 12 costs $10. Which pack is the better buy? Justify your answer.

_____

4 A jar containing 360g of olives costs $8.30 and a larger jar containing 530g costs $13.90.

  a What is the cost of 10g from the smaller jar?

  _____

  b What is the cost of 10g from the larger jar?

  _____

  c Which jar is the better value for money?

  _____

5 Raspberry jam is sold in jars of two sizes. The smaller jar contains 325g and costs $6.24 while the larger jar contains 450g and costs $9.36.

  a What is the cost of 25g from the smaller jar?

  _____

  b What is the cost of 25g from the larger jar?

  _____

  c Which jar is the better value for money? Justify your answer.

  _____

6 A spread consisting of butter and rapeseed oil is sold in packs of two different sizes. The larger pack, which contains 1 kg, sells for $5.80 while the smaller pack, which contains 500 g sells for $4.75.

  a Find the cost of:

    i 100 g from the larger pack

    _____

    ii 100 g from the smaller pack.

    _____

  b Which pack is the better value?

  c Find the amount saved when purchasing 2 kg of the better value pack.

  _____

7 Marlene went to the supermarket for some vegetable oil. She found that the oil she wanted was available in three different sizes. The large 3 litre bottle cost $11.40, the smaller 1 litre bottle $6.50 and the smallest $\frac{1}{2}$ litre bottle $3.30.

  a Which bottle is:

    i the cheapest per 100 ml

    ii the dearest per 100 ml?

  b Marlene decided that the largest of the three sizes was too large for her needs. Which of the other two would you recommend as the best value for money? Justify your answer.

  _____

In questions **8** to **10**, find the total price of the item. Assume that the rate of sales tax is 20%.

8 A freezer marked $1800 + sales tax.

_____

9 A television priced $1250 + sales tax.

_____

10 A three-piece suite costing $12 540 + sales tax.

_____

11 Repeat question **8** but with sales tax of 17.5%. How much less would the freezer cost?

_____

12 A camera was priced $940 plus sales tax at 17.5%

  a What was the price to the buyer?

_____

Some months later the rate of sales tax was increased to 20%.

  b How much more would the camera now cost?

_____

  c Express the increased cost as a percentage of the original purchase price to the buyer.

_____

13 A washing machine is marked $850 plus sales tax at 15%. How much will I have to pay for it?

_____

14 Last month, Rohan saw a computer marked $945 plus sales tax at 15%.

  a How much would the computer cost him?

_____

  b When he eventually decided to buy, the price of the computer had gone down by $50 but sales tax had gone up to 20%. How much more (or less) did Rohan have to pay?

_____

In questions **15** to **18**, find the cash price of the articles following a discount of 20%.

15 An electric mixer marked $95. _____

16 A dress marked $240. _____

17 A set of woodworking tools marked $1250.

_____

18 A sewing machine marked $750.

_____

19 Men's jackets were marked $426. In a sale they were offered at a discount of $33\frac{1}{3}$. What was the discounted price?

_____

In a sale, a ladies' fashion shop offered a discount of 40% on the following articles. Find their sale price.

20 A dress marked $280. _____

21 Shoes at $180 a pair. _____

22 A suit priced $844. _____

23 Skirts at $120 each. _____

24 Trousers at $166 a pair. _____

25 Shoulder bags at $86. _____

In questions **26** to **30**, find the profit or loss.

26 A book bought for $5 and sold for 50c.

_____

27 A set of china bought for $120 and sold for $165.

_____

28 A cricket bat costing $65 and selling at $105.

_____

29 A scanner costing $326 that sold for $421.

_____

30 A telescope bought for $250 and sold for $75.

_____

In questions **31** to **34**, find the percentage profit.

31 Cost price $20, profit $5 _____

32 Cost price $64, profit $19.20 _____

33 Cost price $72, profit $24 _____

34 Cost price $33, profit $3.96 _____

In questions **35** to **38**, find the percentage loss.

35 Cost price $50, loss $10 _____

36 Cost price $250, loss $40 _____

37 Cost price $580, loss $87 _____

38 Cost price $160, loss $64 _____

In questions **39** to **42**, find the selling price.

39 Cost price $740, profit 30% _____

40 Cost price $64, loss 15% _____

41 Cost price $1740, loss 40% _____

42 Cost price $80, profit 60% _____

43 a An article costing $24 is sold to make a profit of $6. Find the percentage profit.

_____

b In a sale, a chair costing the retailer $300 is sold at a loss of $45. Find the percentage loss.

_____

44 Use the given data to find the selling price:

a Cost price $55, profit 24%

_____

b Cost price $64, loss $12\frac{1}{2}$%

_____

c Cost price $145, profit 120%

_____

d Cost price $8500, loss 40%.

_____

45 Assuming that the rate of sales tax is 15% find the purchase price of:

a an electric kettle costing $54 + sales tax

_____

b a tool set costing $120 + sales tax.

_____

46 a In a sale, a shop offered a discount of 30% on a dress marked $140. Find the cash price.

_____

b To get rid of old stock a department store offers a discount of 40% on a jacket marked $165. Find the cash price.

_____

47 Eggs are bought from a farm at $18 for a tray of 36. They are sold at $8.28 per dozen. Find the profit of a dozen eggs as the percentage of the cost price.

_____

48 Find the simple interest on:

a $100 for 3 years at 10% p.a.

_____

b $100 for 5 years at 8% p.a.

_____

c $100 for 2 years at 5% p.a.

_____

d $100 for 8 years at 9% p.a.

_____

e $200 for 4 years at 2% p.a.

_____

f $300 for 6 years at 8% p.a.

_____

g $500 for 7 years at 4% p.a.

_____

h $1000 for 10 years at 13% p.a.

_____

The answers to question **49** are exact in dollars and cents.

49 Find the interest on:

a $450 for 4 years at 3% p.a.

_____

b $175 for 5 years at 4% p.a.

_____

c $244 for 7 years at 6% p.a.

_____

d $382 for 8 years at 11% p.a.

_____

e $736 for 5 years at 8% p.a.

_____

f $992 for 9 years at 12% p.a.

_____

g $455 for 6 years at 9% p.a.

_____

h $542 for 7 years at 5% p.a.

_____

50 Find, giving your answers correct to the nearest cent, the simple interest on:

a $435.52 for 3 years at 6% p.a.

_____

b $176.44 for 7 years at 3% p.a.

_____

c $365.28 for 5 years at 6% p.a.

_____

d $765.40 for 7 years at 9% p.a.

_____

e $123.77 for 4 years at 4% p.a.

_____

f $756.30 for 5 years at 7% p.a.

_____

g $654.88 for 6 years at 9% p.a.

_____

h $727.11 for 8 years at 4% p.a.

_____

51 Find, giving your answers correct to the nearest cent, the simple interest on:

a $176.50 for 3 years at $5\frac{1}{2}$% p.a.

_____

b $303.60 for $2\frac{1}{2}$ years at 9% p.a.

_____

c $78.43 for 5 years at 5% p.a.

_____

d $175.66 for $4\frac{1}{4}$ years at $3\frac{3}{4}$% p.a.

_____

e $505.54 for 7 years at $10\frac{1}{2}$% p.a.

_____

f $645.88 for $3\frac{3}{4}$ years at $7\frac{1}{4}$% p.a.

_____

g $254.54 for 5 years at $4\frac{1}{2}$% p.a.

_____

h $345.43 for 4 years at $8\frac{3}{4}$% p.a.

_____

52 Find, giving your answers correct to the nearest cent, the simple interest on:

a $250 for 100 days at 8% p.a.

_____

b $354 for 200 days at 4% p.a.

_____

c $254.75 for 67 days at 5% p.a.

_____

d $456.74 for 86 days at $9\frac{1}{2}$% p.a.

_____

53 Find, giving answers that are not exact correct to the nearest cent, the amount of:

a $250 for 4 years at 10% p.a.

_____

b $750 for 8 years at 6% p.a.

_____

c $344 for 5 years at 3% p.a.

_____

d $526.50 for 6 years at $4\frac{1}{2}$% p.a.

_____

e $318.55 for 3 years at 8% p.a.

_____

f $657.40 for $4\frac{1}{2}$ years at $9\frac{1}{4}$% p.a.

_____

g $824 for 7 years at $5\frac{3}{4}$% p.a.

_____

h $335.33 for $6\frac{1}{2}$ years at $11\frac{1}{2}$% p.a.

_____

54 Find the principal that will earn:

a $140 simple interest in 4 years at 5% p.a.

_____

b $84 simple interest in 5 years at 3% p.a.

_____

c $336 simple interest in 7 years at 8% p.a.

_____

d $216.45 simple interest in $4\frac{1}{2}$ years at $6\frac{1}{2}$% p.a.

_____

e $718.41 simple interest in $5\frac{1}{2}$ years at $10\frac{1}{2}$% p.a.

_____

55 What is the rate per cent if the cost of borrowing:

a $400 for 5 years is $80

_____

b $750 for 4 years is $150

_____

c $500 for 8 years is $340

_____

d $650 for 3 years is $87.75

e $240 for 6 years is $104.40?

56 What is the rate per cent if:

a $300 will earn $54 simple interest in 3 years

b $450 will earn $180 simple interest in 5 years

c $740 will earn $133.20 simple interest in 6 years

d $530 will earn $79.50 simple interest in 2 years

e $870 will earn $382.80 simple interest in 4 years?

57 Find the number of years in which:

a $200 invested at 5% p.a. simple interest will earn $50

b $350 invested at 7% p.a. simple interest will earn $98

c $480 invested at 12% p.a. simple interest will earn $345.60

d $355 invested at 8% p.a. simple interest will earn $85.20

e $844 invested at 9% p.a. simple interest will earn $379.80

f $672 invested at 4% p.a. simple interest will earn $147.84.

58 What sum of money will amount to:

a $330 if invested for 2 years at 5% p.a.

b $558 if invested for 3 years at 8% p.a.

c $954 if invested for 5 years at $6\frac{1}{2}$ % p.a.

d $1297.20 if invested for 4 years at $9\frac{1}{2}$% p.a.?

59 Complete the following table:

Principal in $	Rate % p.a.	Time	Simple interest in $	Amount in $
350	6	4 years		
534		5 years	213.60	
750	7			907.50
	10		336	756
820		9 months	49.20	

60 Carlton Fullerton borrows a sum of money from his bank for 8 months at 9% per annum simple interest. If this loan costs him $45 how much does he borrow?

61 If $360 amounts to $398.40 in 8 months, to what will it amount, at the same rate of interest, in 1 year?

62 Mrs Alcott's bank pays interest at $4\frac{1}{2}$% p.a. on money she has deposited with them. How much is in her account if the simple interest for 9 months is $27?

63 The interest received on $1460 is $24 when it is invested for a certain number of days at 2%. For how many days was the sum invested?

64 Desmond Savage borrowed $584 at 12% p.a. When he repaid the debt the interest due was $17.28. For how many days did he borrow the money?

65 When a firm borrowed a large sum of money, the interest rate was 14% p.a., and was to be paid monthly. After 5 months the rate of interest dropped by $1\frac{1}{2}$% p.a., causing the monthly interest payment to go down by $18.75. Work out the sum of money borrowed.

Review test 3: units 14 to 21

In questions **1** to **10**, choose the letter that gives the correct answer.

1 45% of 0.06 is:

| **A** 0.27 | **B** 0.027 |
| **C** 0.0027 | **D** none of these |

2 0.006 km expressed in centimetres is:

| **A** 0.6 cm | **B** 6 cm |
| **C** 60 cm | **D** 600 cm |

3 The difference, in square centimetres, in the area of a rectangle measuring 8 cm by 12 mm and a square of side 3 cm is:

| **A** 0.6 | **B** 6 |
| **C** 60 | **D** 87 |

4 The next two numbers in the sequence 10, 2, 0.4, 0.08 are:

| **A** 0.0032 and 0.016 | **B** 0.08 and 0.016 |
| **C** 0.016 and 0.0032 | **D** 0.016 and 0.008 |

5 Black cartridges for Abb's computer are sold in four sizes.

Size **A** costs $52.99 and should yield 1200 pages of print.

Size **B** costs $39.99 and should yield 800 pages of print.

Size **C** costs $31.80 and should yield 450 pages of print.

Size **D** costs $16.99 and should yield 225 pages of print.

Which size gives the best value for money?

| **A** | **B** | **C** | **D** |

6 The most suitable unit to measure the mass of one of the tablets Joe was prescribed by the doctor is:

| **A** milligrams | **B** grams | **C** kilograms |

7 The number of grams in 474 mg is

| **A** 47.4 | **B** 4.74 |
| **C** 0.474 | **D** 0.0474 |

8 The number of axes of symmetry a square has is:

| **A** 1 | **B** 2 |
| **C** 3 | **D** 4 |

9 The number of axes of symmetry a rhombus has is:

| **A** 1 | **B** 2 |
| **C** 3 | **D** 4 |

10 The value of x that satisfies the equation $3(x + 2) - 4(3 - 2x) = 16$ is:

| **A** 1 | **B** 2 |
| **C** 3 | **D** $4\frac{2}{5}$ |

11 Express each percentage as a fraction in its lowest terms:

a 75% _____

b 68% _____

c 170% _____

12 Express the following percentages as decimals:

a 84% _____

b 26% _____

c $62\frac{1}{2}$% _____

13 Express the following fractions as percentages, giving answers correct to one decimal place where necessary:

a $\frac{17}{20}$ _____

b $\frac{5}{12}$ _____

c $1\frac{5}{8}$ _____

14 Express the following decimals as percentages:

   a 0.16   _____

   b 0.95   _____

   c 1.78   _____

15 Express:

   a 25 cm as a percentage of 2 m

   _____

   b 2400 g as a percentage of 3648 g.

   _____

16 Find:

   a 34% of $750

   _____

   b 58% of 23600 km.

   _____

17 In a sale, an article was reduced from $540 to $450. Find:

   a the reduction in the price

   _____

   b the percentage reduction on the original price.

   _____

18 In a sale, the price of an article marked at $1480 is reduced by 30%. Find the sale price.

   _____

19 Dried fruit bought at $88 per 50 kg bag is sold at $2.42 per kilogram. Find the profit.

   _____

20 A shopkeeper buys 300 articles for $2400 and sells them at $7 each. Find his loss.

   _____

21 Express:

   a 5 cm 5 mm in millimetres _____

   b 5 t 384 kg in kilograms   _____

   c 0.06 kg in grams   _____

   d 34 g in milligrams   _____

   e 0.042 km in metres.   _____

22 Express:

   a 3 m + 36 cm in metres   _____

   b 745 m + 0.65 km in kilometres _____

   c 645 mm + 52 cm + 2 m in metres _____

   d 1 t + 750 kg in tonnes.   _____

23 Express 0.645 m in:

   a centimetres   _____

   b millimetres   _____

   c kilometres.   _____

24 The perimeter of a rectangle is 54.6 cm.

   a The length of one side is 13.3 cm. Is this one of the long sides? Justify your answer.

   _____

   b Find the dimensions of the rectangle.

   _____

25 Given that 1 metre ≈ 39 inches how much longer or shorter is 440 yards than 400 metres?

   _____

26 In training, an athlete runs 100 laps around a 400 m track. He estimates that he has run about 5 miles. Is he correct? Justify your answer.

   _____

27 The length of one side of a square is 40.25 cm. Calculate the perimeter of the square:

   a in centimetres   _____

   b in metres   _____

28 A tin of tomatoes has a mass of 235 g. What is the mass, in kilograms, of a carton of 72 of these tins?

_____

29 Find, giving your answer in the unit in brackets:

   a 5 × 3 kg 467 g (g)   _____

   b 6 × 7 cm 3 mm (cm)   _____

   c 8 × 3 km 420 m (m)   _____

30 Find, giving your answer in the unit in brackets:

   a 8 yd 1 ft (ft)   _____

   b 5 ft 3 in (in)   _____

   c 3 miles 266 yd (yd)   _____

31 Find, giving your answer in the unit in brackets:

   a 2 cwt 60 lb (lb)   _____

   b 5 tons 12 cwt (cwt)   _____

   c 24 oz (lb and oz)   _____

32 Which is the shorter journey and by how many kilometres?

   a A journey of 12 miles.

   b A journey of 19 km.

_____

33 Penny went on a 12-day holiday on 9 June.

   a How many nights was she away?

_____

   b What date did she return?

_____

34 **a** Write 135 minutes in hours and minutes.

_____

   b Write 300 hours in days and hours.

_____

35 Tim's football match began at 10.15 a.m. The playing time was 90 minutes. There was a 10 minute break at half-time and 4 minutes was added because of stoppages during the game. What time did Tim's match finish?

_____

36 How many hours and minutes are there between 9.15 p.m. and 3.15 p.m. the following day?

_____

37 The time needed to cook a joint of meat is 25 minutes per pound plus 20 minutes. How long should it take to cook a $3\frac{1}{2}$ lb joint?

_____

38 Find the period of time between:

   a 0730 hours and 1415 on the same day

_____

   b 0845 hours and 1615 the same day

_____

   c 2145 hours and 0930 the next day.

_____

39 Convert:

   a 67 in into ft and in   _____

   b 10000 yd into miles and yd   _____

   c 7 ft 6 in into in   _____

   d 9 yd 2 ft into ft   _____

40 Write the first unit roughly in terms of the unit in brackets.

  a 9 lb (kg)   _____

  b 250 g (oz)   _____

  c 7 m (ft)   _____

  d 3.5 kg (lb)   _____

41 At the market I buy a 2 kg bag of sugar, a 3 kg bag of flour and a 5 lb bag of mixed vegetables. What mass in pounds, roughly, do I have to carry home?

_____

42 For each shape draw the axis of symmetry.

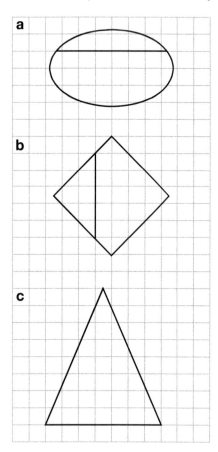

43 Draw the axes of symmetry for these shapes.

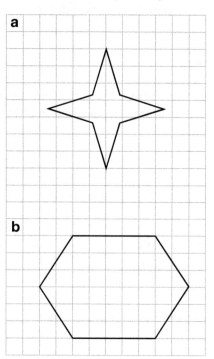

44 How many axes of symmetry does each of these letters have?

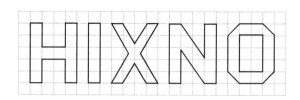

H _____

I _____

X _____

N _____

O _____

45 Complete each drawing so the broken line is an axis of symmetry.

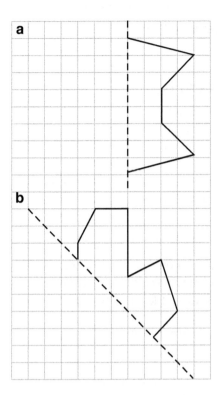

46 Complete this drawing so that each broken line is an axis of symmetry.

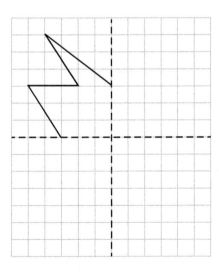

47 Find the area of a square of side 3.4 cm, stating clearly the units of your answer.

_____

48 Find the area of a rectangle measuring 1.6 m by 4.3 m, stating clearly the units of your answer.

_____

49 The perimeter of a rectangle is 56 cm. If it is 16 cm long find:

  a its width   _____

  b its area.   _____

50 The area of a rectangle is 18 cm². If it is 5 cm long find:

  a its breadth   _____

  b its perimeter.   _____

51 Express:

  a 1400 mm² in cm²   _____

  b 0.0066 m² in cm²   _____

  c 58 cm² in mm².   _____

52 Express:

  a 312000 m² in km²   _____

  b 0.0047 m² in cm²   _____

  c 180 cm² in mm².   _____

In questions **53** to **56**, find the area of each rectangle, giving your answer in the unit in brackets.

53 length 3.5 m, breadth 0.3 m (cm²)

_____

54 length 5.5 cm, breadth 2.8 cm (mm²)

_____

55 length 0.36 m, breadth 0.24 m (cm²)

_____

56 length 0.14 km, breadth 0.025 km (m²)

_____

In questions **57** and **58**, find the area of the given shape. All measurements are in centimetres.

57

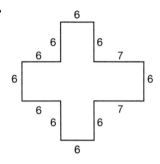

_____

58

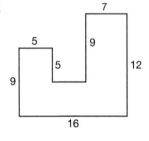

_____

59 Find the area of this triangle.

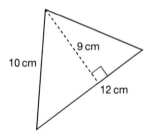

_____

60 The diagram shows a rectangular sheet of card measuring 9 cm by 8 cm. The sheet is cut up into five triangles A, B, C, D, E. Find the area of each triangle. All measurements are in centimetres.

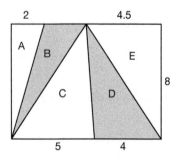

Area of triangle A

_____

Area of triangle B

_____

Area of triangle C

_____

Area of triangle D

_____

Area of triangle E

_____

61 Three building bricks are laid ontop of each other and reach a height of 215 mm. Each brick is separated by a layer of cement 10 mm thick.

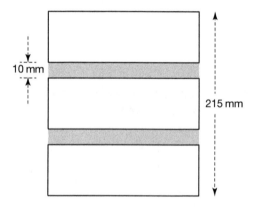

a Find the thickness of one brick.

_____

b Find the dimensions of a brick if its thickness is two-thirds its width and it is twice as long as it is wide.

_____

c A wall is built to a height of 2.25 m by laying all the bricks longways. How many courses are needed? (Assume that the thickness of cement under the first brick and under each course is 10 mm.)

_____

62 A wooden door has three glass panels, as shown in the diagram.

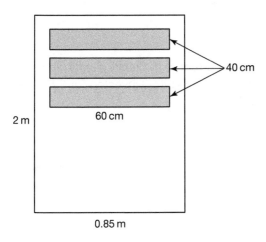

40 cm

2 m

60 cm

0.85 m

Find:

a the area of each panel

b the area of wood in the door.

In questions **63** to **67**, solve the given equation.

63 a $7 + x = 20$

  b $e - 7 = 7$

  c $8 - b = 4$

64 a $3x - 4 = 8$

  b $7 = 5a - 13$

  c $3x + 9 = 9$

65 $7 + 2x - 3(x - 1) = 4$

66 $4x + 3 + 5(2 - x) = 5$

67 $6(x + 2) - 5(2x - 3) - 2(4x - 5) = 5$

68 Find three consecutive whole numbers such that their sum is 96.

69 Three consecutive even numbers are such that the sum of the largest and the smallest is 108. Find the three numbers.

70 I think of a number, multiply it by 3 and add 7. The result is 19. What number did I think of?

71 Write the next two terms in each of the following sequences:

  a 2, 5, 10,

  b −3, −8, −13,

  c 0.4, 0.2, 0.1,

72 The nth term of a sequence is $8n - 3$. Write the first three terms and the 10th term.

73 The nth term of a sequence is $10 - 2n$. Write the first three terms and the 10th term.

74 The nth term of a sequence is $4(7 - 4n)$. Write the first three terms and the 10th term.

75 Ball-point pens are sold in packs of six or ten. A six-pack costs \$4 whereas a ten-pack costs \$6. Which is the better buy? Justify your answer.

76 The price of a washing machine is \$890 plus sales tax at 20%. How much will the washing machine cost me?

77 The marked price of a tablecloth is \$85 but in a sale it is offered at a discount of 20%. Find the discounted price.

78 A china dog, whose marked price is $475, is offered in a sale at a discount of 30%. How much will it cost me?

79 Find the price of a T-shirt marked $70 but offered, in a sale, at a discount of 40%.

80 Find the price of a shredder marked $145 but offered at a discount of 40% in a sale.

81 An article bought by a retailer for $56 is sold for $70. Find:

a the profit

b the profit as a percentage of the price paid by the retailer.

82 Mr Ali buys a wooden desk for $875. He sells it at a profit of 30%. Find the selling price.

83 Find the simple interest on $700 invested for 3 years at 4% p.a.

84 Find, correct to the nearest cent, the simple interest on $542.50 invested for 5 years at 3% p.a.

85 Find, correct to the nearest cent, the simple interest on $764.50 invested for $3\frac{1}{2}$ years at $3\frac{3}{4}$% p.a.

86 Find the principal that will earn $171 simple interest in 3 years at 6% p.a.

87 What is the rate per cent, if the cost of borrowing $900 for 5 years is $180?

88 How many years will it take for $875 to earn $175 at 4% p.a simple interest?

89 Find the principal that will earn $130 simple interest in 4 years at 5% p.a.

90 What sum of money will amount to $1652 if invested for 3 years at 6% p.a.?